Introduction

Out of all the walking guides available on the books
will select ours (maybe you already have!). But why
already have several such books gathering dust at hc

We set out to make this one a little different. It consists of twelve thoroughly
researched walks (plus two optional extensions) all based around fairly close, but
distinct, areas of the Peak - the four villages of Eyam, Grindleford, Ashford in the
Water and Hathersage. Each walk has a great deal to offer in terms of beauty,
variety and points of interest, and we feel confident that the first one you attempt
will encourage you to walk the others.

We have taken immense care to make the route instructions clear and totally
confusion free, so that although simple maps are provided, these are intended only
as general indicators of the point you have reached on the route. Nor is it assumed
that you will carry an Ordnance Survey map, although starting point grid
references are given. The instructions have all been very carefully checked, and
friends have generously given their time and energy to walk the routes in order to
ensure there are no areas of uncertainty. It is, though, important to remember that
the countryside is a living environment, so changes can occur. A stile, for example,
may be replaced with a gate, etc. Particular points of interest are highlighted on
each walk and we hope these will add to your enjoyment.

These circular walks vary in length and in terrain and the general summary before
each one will help you to make your choice. In the beautiful Derbyshire
countryside it is very difficult to avoid the occasional hill, and we are assuming
our walkers are of normal health and fitness (let's mention here that we are both
well into middle age!). Because many surfaces are uneven and certain areas can
sometimes be muddy, lightweight walking boots are recommended for all our
walks (if you succeed in persuading teenagers along with you, warn them against
expensive designer trainers!).

But the walks are not all we hope you will get from this book. For each of the four
villages, around which the walks are located, there is a short narrative. This is set
in an interesting time of that particular village's history, and although the narrator
of each one is a fictional character, the general details of the historical setting are
researched and accurate. Four very different people, with contrasting lives, tell
their own stories. We hope you will take even greater pleasure in walking each area
after reading these tales.

This book has been hard work, but we have thoroughly enjoyed both walking and
writing it. Our great wish is that you enjoy it too!

Contents

Eyam

Grindleford

Ashford in the Water

Hathersage

The Eyam Walks

Mompesson's Well

Café

Roman Baths

The Plague Woman's Tale

Does our village look lovely to you now? How quaint, how idyllic! Charming even on a damp and overcast day. Some of you no doubt believe that you would like to live in such a place, perhaps raise young children here, or find in it a retreat for old age? It is heavy with memories, preserved almost perfectly in time, holding the essence of Old England.

But be thankful that your eyes never opened upon this village when I, as a young woman, lived here. Looking back upon my childhood I remember it fondly, as a place filled with down-to-earth people of character, of toughness, of generosity. Yet it was hard and unyielding, a windswept cluster of homes surrounded by desolate hills, where the weather was so often harsh, where earning the means of survival was a demanding task, faced grindingly each day. In the steep sloping fields where I often toiled as a girl, or in the watery gloom of the lead mine where Thomas laboured, life offered nothing of ease or comfort.

Yet how much more we might have treasured our simple means of survival, our youth, our health, had we glimpsed what was to come.

As I approached the age of nineteen and Thomas reached twenty, God began to punish our village for what surely must have been some terrible sins. It began abruptly, and it was Thomas himself who brought me the first piece of news. After his usual labours (never would I have exchanged the chill open fields for those dank caverns) he came, as so often, to our small and slightly crumbling farmhouse for some broth. The word 'farmhouse' exaggerates its size. It was, like many others, but a substantial cottage at the edge of a few acres of smallholding, a little under a mile from the village centre. This distance, often seeming inconvenient to me as a child, was probably to prove my salvation, and that of my father. My mother had died in childbirth some six years before, taking with her my infant brother. Naturally I had long been expected, as the only daughter, to occupy her place in all matters of housekeeping. My help was required in no less a measure outside, where hens, ducks, a few sheep and a crop of oats provided scantily for most of our needs. In his own interest, father would probably have preferred me never to marry. Nevertheless he seemed to like Thomas, to whom I had promised my hand, and made him as welcome as his own taciturn soul would allow. Thomas was far stronger and abler than my brother, two years my senior, and a reliable source of practical help when the elements turned viciously against us.

That evening, early in September 1665 (how could the season, the year, not be etched deep into my memory?) Thomas told us that George Viccars was dead. I should explain to you that George was a tailor, who seemed to have travelled quite widely in the country and who had for some time been lodging with Mary Cooper - once a close friend of my mother - in her cottage at the heart of the village. Faces changed little at that time, and a stranger's face was always an object of curiosity. Many had made themselves acquainted with George, had been fascinated by his travels. He had connections with the London cloth trade, a fact that was to prove the trap door through which we would fall to our misery. Only later was this known, of course. Only later were stories passed around that cloth he had received in a box from that city, which was hung on a rail to air, was the carrier of disease.

Naturally there was sorrow at the news of his death, which had apparently happened quickly, following a brief but violent illness. George had endured a raging fever, had screamed at the pain in his head. His body had been shaking uncontrollably and bathed in foul smelling sweat. Beneath his arms strange and grossly engorged lumps had suddenly appeared, a livid red colour.

Such ills were not unheard of by certain older members of our community. Despite this and the whispered horror of his state, we were as yet unsuspecting of what was to come.

Within no less than a few days, three of George's neighbours were dead, each of them suffering the same bodily agonies as he himself had endured. Fear began to spread through the people of our village as we sensed a growing, malign danger to us all. My father, with an instinctive wisdom, bade me stay within the confines of our house and its fields. I did not long do so. Just sixteen days later, in early October, I heard that a childhood friend lay dying. As I stood at the doorway of her stench filled room, uttering a prayer with her distraught mother, I begged God to have mercy on her, and upon us all.

No fewer than twenty-three people of our village died that month. Mary Cooper's three-year-old son, Edward, was amongst them and her five-year-old Jonathon was lost to her just ten days later. How she must have cursed the day she took a lodger into her home! Grief and terror were now in the very air we breathed. My father did not forbid Thomas to visit us and he came each evening, so that we both might be reassured of the other's continuing good health. Daily now we became aware of new illness, of rapid death, of hysterical scenes of grief. No longer did we talk of our future, our marriage, but only grasped at the presence of each other in that moment.

Those who were able were already leaving this place of disease and death. Their number included, unsurprisingly, the land owning Sheldons, the family of Bradshaw Hall and others whose means afforded them some independence of action. Most of us had nowhere to go, no easy means of earning a living beyond our village and its farmland, where almost all had lived from birth. My father did not even consider such a solution. A deeply religious and inward looking man, he held little fear of death and believed we should continue to work, to pray, to put our trust in God and take what fate awaited us. Thomas had cousins in Baslow and could perhaps have gone to them. He did not. For this I have felt a heavy burden of guilt throughout my life.

I now know that our village was not unique in its suffering. Over the years, other villages and many towns had been similarly visited. But as grief and panic engulfed us, our people took actions that were special, indeed that were, as far as I am aware, unknown before or since. If you suspect we did so because we were people of special courage, you would be quite wrong. We did this because we had living in the village two men of quite exceptional character.

Mr Mompesson was our church minister, stricken by what he was witnessing around him, desperately anxious for the safety of his wife and young children. I was told he begged

Catherine to leave. She would not, but finally agreed to send the children to safety in North Yorkshire. She remained with him, supporting and comforting the sick and bereaved, especially the children who could not, unlike her own, be sent to safety. Her husband, however, sensed that more was needed than acts of mercy, that far more was demanded than prayer. Whether God moved within him I do not know. At that time he was quite a young man, not yet thirty, in addition to being fairly new to our parish. He was not therefore a natural leader for us during this terrifying time. Mercifully he was helped and guided by the previous incumbent, the Puritan minister Mr. Stanley, who was at that time living in the village. The two now knew it was vital to bury the differences of religious view which had previously divided them so deeply, to speak to us with one voice.

In the June of that terrible year of 1666 these two men faced the people of our village together. They had decided on a course of action, one that was not intended to save us, indeed one which would make us all prisoners within this pit of disease. What we heard from their mouths was hard indeed. What they asked of us was more than should be demanded of simple people.

Until such time as God lifted this terrible curse from us, no person would move beyond agreed village boundaries (within which my own dwelling lay). We would no longer gather in large groups, which risked further spread of disease. Therefore from that day the church would be locked and no further funerals would take place. Families and neighbours must bury the dead, as quickly as possible after their demise and at good depth.

There was, of course, deep distress at such suggestions. Most had not the means of fleeing, yet cherished their freedom to do so. To bury loved ones without church ceremony, to cast them hastily into makeshift graves, was horrifying to religious minds. There was deep concern also about the wherewithal of our survival, even if such survival was to be temporary. The village was not self-supporting, its appalling death toll making it less so as each day passed. How would we be fed? This vital question, however, had already been considered by the two gentlemen, who had called upon the generosity of the Duke at Chatsworth. Food and other essentials could be brought for us and left at certain agreed points along our outer boundaries.

To provide comfort and mutual support, a religious service would be held weekly in the open. The place chosen for this was the Delph, a large but enclosed 'basin' close to the village centre where some form of worship could take place, but in which families would be able to stand well apart. All of us would undertake to remain in this village, to be its willing prisoners. By doing this we would perhaps safeguard the lives of others beyond our boundaries. We would be doing a Holy thing. We would be Blessed.

There was much anguish. There was some anger. There were tears and there was blaspheming. But finally we agreed.

Confinement within our own boundaries began at once. Rules were abided by in almost all respects, but we were human. Some of us were young, and felt the terror of both life and love being ripped from us. Another childhood friend of mine, Emmot Sidall, had planned to marry a young man in the neighbouring village of Stoney Middleton. Throughout that terrible winter of 1665 to 1666 he had come each day to the village to ensure that she was well. Finally, she begged him not to endanger his life anymore. However, unbeknown to

Emmot's widowed mother, who had lost her husband and five children by the end of 1665, the couple continued to meet on occasions in the more sheltered fringes of the Delph. But the birth of spring was cruel. The poor girl fell ill and died towards the end of April and Rowland waited for her many times in vain. It appears that no-one let him know, but in the horror of that time people faced grief and loss on every side and all of us were stricken. Emmot's mother, Elizabeth, had remarried just five days before Emmot was so cruelly taken. Sadly, her new husband was to follow his stepdaughter to the grave in July.

I know that Rowland was one of the first to enter the village when the curse of disease was finally lifted from us. He must in his heart have known what news awaited him, but it seems he had not quite extinguished hope.

As midsummer of 1666 approached, death gathered pace and strength. Neither youth nor health offered any protection and those of us who remained well grew more certain each day that we too must finally be doomed. My brother, always lazy and inadequate, became more so, offering precious little help on the farm, retreating into solitude and stupor. Against my father's will he visited the owners of the Miners Arms, an inn now unused by the villagers.

Was it there that the hand of death touched his shoulder? We buried him two days after that first fever, my father and Thomas dragging his blackening corpse, wrapped in an old sheet, to the furthest corner of our land. I wept, but my grief was small against that which ravaged me just three weeks later.

Thomas failed to appear at the farm around his usual hour. Aware that he had seemed exhausted the previous day, and had barely eaten, I was thrown into panic. Rushing down towards the far side of the village, I entered the worker's cottage he shared with his widowed mother. I found her struck silent, motionless, suffering a grief too great for her mind to bear. Thomas had fallen ill the previous evening, not two hours after leaving me. Throughout the night, his mother later told me, she had tried to minister to his unquenchable thirst, to wipe the blood seeping from his nostrils and mouth, to calm his delirious ramblings. Death had taken him with even more savage speed than was usual and he had died just after midday.

Already her neighbours had dragged his still warm body up the rough track beside the cottage and had buried it in the oat field beyond. She could not walk there with me. I walked alone. Standing by the rough overturned earth, I thanked God that his suffering had not been prolonged.

Grieving was the normality of my life and of the lives of everyone around me. No longer did any horror shock. When I heard that Mrs Hancock, a good, kind woman, had lost her husband and her five children, and that the sixth lay dying, I remained almost unmoved, quite unable to shed a tear, too numbed even to utter a prayer. Perhaps such numbness is God's way of preserving us against what might otherwise overwhelm and destroy. Mrs Hancock, who lived at the eastern end of the village, dragged each one of her family from her home to a nearby place, a bleak hillside spot known as Riley. Within a mere six days all seven had died and had been roughly, unceremoniously buried by her own poor hands. I believe she then fled in her grief to Sheffield, to spend the rest of her days with her one remaining son, who worked there in the cutlery trade. Surely no one could condemn such an escape? Only now do I see clearly the horrors God willed her to endure.

She was, nonetheless, luckier in her flight than another, a desperate woman who tried to flee unnoticed to Tideswell on that town's market day. She was pelted with stones and driven back by terrified villagers, then to face the anger and scorn of our own people.

I no longer even attempted to confine myself to the farm, but used my energies to be of practical help to others. Often I walked to one boundary point or another to collect the provisions generously left there (though no doubt it was a price others felt to be worth paying in exchange for our isolation). For certain things, such as materials, coins needed to be passed across. These I would drop into a small hole, gouged into the surface of the boundary stone and filled with cleansing vinegar.

We came to respect our minister increasingly, all the more so after his wife's death in mid-summer. His obvious grief did not long deter him from his tasks of comfort, support, of organisation. Those of us who lived did not go hungry and we were not let down by the ones who had promised him to supply us with food. I understand that much later, and in another place, he married once again and I hope that he was rewarded with happiness.

In the autumn of that terrible year of 1666, God decided we had endured enough. Whatever evil had been done in this place, we had paid for it with our suffering. It seems now that the last death from this terrible curse took place on the first day of November, though naturally we did not realise this to be the case until much later. August and September had been terrible, cruel months with more than a hundred deaths. The fall to 14 deaths in October had raised hopes only slightly. Such hope had been raised, and cruelly dashed, before.

Slowly, as November progressed into deep winter, I allowed myself to believe I might survive. To many though, the mere fact of survival was not cause for joy or celebration. Some had lost every person they had ever loved and older people, in particular, knew they would never recover. Their losses were too savagely complete. But, gradually and fearfully, others appeared in this place, usually seeking news of a distant relative.

Mr Mompesson, in his wisdom, encouraged us all to burn our clothes, our furniture and bedding, and huge bonfires could regularly be seen in and around the village. Perhaps we should have made fires earlier. Perhaps we should have destroyed our very homes, and lived, as indeed a few did, in simple huts on the hills.

Be that as it may, some accumulation of pain was now eased in the lighting of fires, in the crackling sounds of hungry flames. The few remaining young started to grasp at excitement once again. Life will not for too long be held down.

This tale has gone on long enough. Take a walk around our village and beyond. Visit the beautiful Church, once locked to us. Look at the cottages, such appealing places, once the containers of pain, of fear, of death. Visit the simple graves of poor Mrs Hancock's family, just a few graves among so very many, most of the others unmarked. If you decide to walk as far as Stoney Middleton, think of Emmot and Rowland, of their doomed love. By our actions, I believe we saved the lives of those who lived in that place, whose boundary lies so close to our own.

There are beautiful and interesting things to see as you walk, far more than I have been able to mention. Enjoy them......... and be grateful!

Look out for these, which you will pass on our Eyam Walks!

Eyam Museum - just opposite the car park. A small but interesting museum, based mainly upon the plague that ravaged the village in the 17th century.
Open Easter - October, Tuesday to Sunday, and Bank Holiday Mondays.
For more information ring 01433 631371.

Stocks - opposite Eyam Hall. Probably used for the punishment of lead miners found guilty of offences by the Barmote Court. The Barmote Court was established around 700 years ago to deal with disputes arising in the lead mining industry and to collect the royalties due to the Crown or the Church.

Eyam Hall - very attractive and interesting manor house built in 1671, with gardens and adjoining craft centre and café. The Hall has been the home of the Wright family for over 300 years. Guided tours are available - open end of June to 1st September.
For more information ring 01433 631976.

Plague Cottages - don't miss this row of terraced cottages in Church Street. The first death from the plague, that of a travelling tailor called George Viccars, took place in one of these and other victims rapidly followed (see plaques on cottages). It is believed the virus came to the village in a box of cloth sent to him from London, which was found to be damp on arrival. George Viccars had the cloth hung up to air, almost certainly releasing disease ridden fleas, although the connection between fleas and plague was not made at the time.

Bagshaw House - opposite the 'plague cottages'. Emmot Sidall, betrothed to a man in Stoney Midddleton, died here during the plague along with other members of her family. Her betrothed was one of the first to enter the village after the plague had ended, only to have his hopes of her survival dashed.

Parish Church of St. Lawrence - well worth a short visit, it partly dates from the 12th century and probably stands on a Saxon foundation. In the churchyard is a well preserved Saxon Cross and also the grave of Catherine Mompesson, a plague victim and wife of the minister who played such an active role in ensuring the village's isolation during that time. The church contains a very informative display relating to the plague.

Bull's Head - former inn, now private apartments, note information plaque on wall.

Bull Ring - original ring, now in the village square, dating from the era of bull baiting.

Miners Arms - 17th century inn, often used as a meeting place for the Barmote Court, which oversaw the conduct of lead miners. Reputed as the most haunted pub in Derbyshire.

Mompesson's Well - one of a number of boundary points, at which food and other essentials were left for the village people, at the time of the plague. This made it possible for them to remain isolated from the outside world. Coins were sometimes left by the villagers, soaking in vinegar in holes gouged out of the stones.

Royal Oak Inn, Merrill Cottage, Richard Furness' House, West End Cottage and Town Head Factory - all these buildings are important in the village's history and have interesting information plaques. They can all be viewed on Walk 2.

Walk I

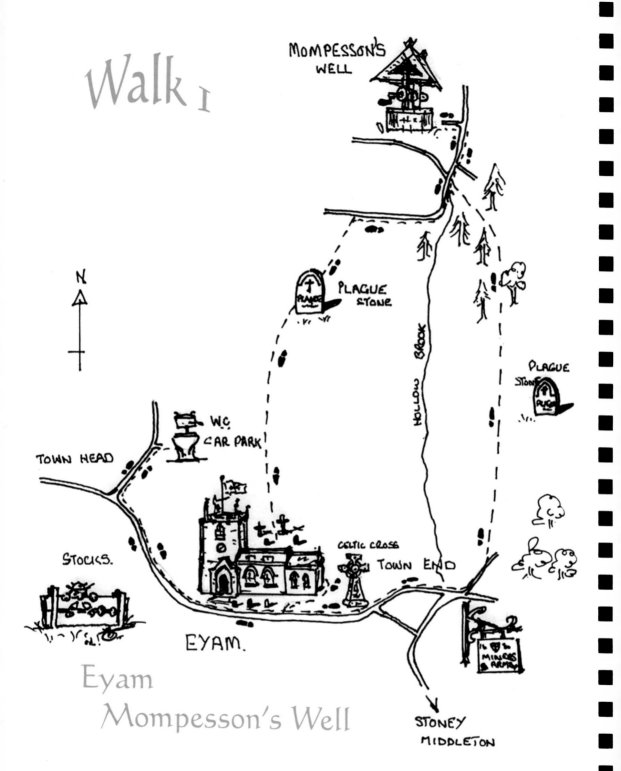

MOMPESSON'S WELL

N

PLAGUE STONE

PLAGUE STONE

HOLLOW BROOK

W.C CAR PARK

TOWN HEAD

STOCKS.

CELTIC CROSS

TOWN END

EYAM.

STONEY MIDDLETON

Eyam
Mompesson's Well

Walk 1

Eyam Village - Mompesson's Well

About this walk

This is a fairly short walk - about an hour - but the village itself includes so many points of historical interest that you may find you want to allow quite a bit longer. Perhaps you might also consider combining this walk with a visit to Eyam Hall, the Parish Church or the village museum. If you would like a longer walk, this one can be linked easily to Walk 3 (to Stoney Middleton). There are good views, both on the way up to the well and on the return. At the well itself there is a bench, ideal for a breather and a few moments reflection on the devastating plague of 1665-6. Provisions were left here for the villagers to enable them to remain in isolation.

Distance	3.3km.
Terrain	There is a steepish ascent from the village up through the wood, but after this stage of the walk, the way is either level or downhill. Parts of the return section can be extra wet and muddy after rainy periods.
Map	OS Explorer OL24 The Peak District, White Peak area. 1:25 000 scale.
Starting Point	Eyam car park on Hawkhill Road, off Church Street (pay and display). Church Street is the main street running through Eyam village. Grid reference SK 216 767.
Refreshments	Eyam has several attractive pubs, teashops and cafés offering a range of drinks, snacks and meals.

✓ *Before leaving car park, have a look at information board near the entrance giving a concise history of the village.*

1. From car park entrance turn *left* into **Hawkhill Road** and walk down to T-junction

2. At T-junction turn *left* into **Church Street** and follow it through village

✓ *See details of historic points of interest on page 9 and look out for information plaques on walls throughout the village.*

3. When you reach **The Square** (where there are a number of cafés and shops) take a short detour to the *left* into **Water Lane** to view **Miners Arms** and information plaque

4. Then return to **The Square**, turn *left* onto **The Causeway** and head up the hill

5. After approximately 150m turn *left* into **Riley Back Lane**

6. Just inside **Riley Back Lane** bear *right* up hill (lane soon becomes path, wall on left)

7. At about 100m up hill, ignore path to left, keep heading up main path into wood

8. Keep walking up path for about 300m until you reach the road

9. When you meet road turn *right* (quiet road with no pavement, so take care on this short section) and ignore road to your left, signposted to Bretton, Gt. Hucklow, Foolow

10. Approximately 150m up road, on your left, is **Mompesson's Well** (just off road)

✓ When the village was struck by plague in the years 1665-6, the villagers opted to remain in isolation in order to contain its spread. To enable them to do this, food, medication and other items were left at a number of boundary points around the village, of which this well was one. It is named after the church minister of the time.

11. On leaving the well, turn **right** and follow road down hill, again ignoring turning, this time on your right

12. Carry on downhill, straight past **Hollowbrook Barn** (ignoring opening to woodland path that you came up)

13. Continue down road for about 300m, passing some railings on your left as road crosses river. Soon after railings (approximately 130m) go through small gate on left into field

14. Keep to path on your right and follow it down as it becomes steps

15. Go through small gate at bottom of steps, turn **left** and carry on down, with wall on left

16. At bottom of field you will see gateposts ahead and a small stile to the right. Cross through stile and follow lane down to graveyard

17. Enter graveyard through gate, walk through and exit graveyard onto **Church Street**

18. Turn **right** and follow **Church Street** back to **Hawkhill Road** and car park

Plague Cottages

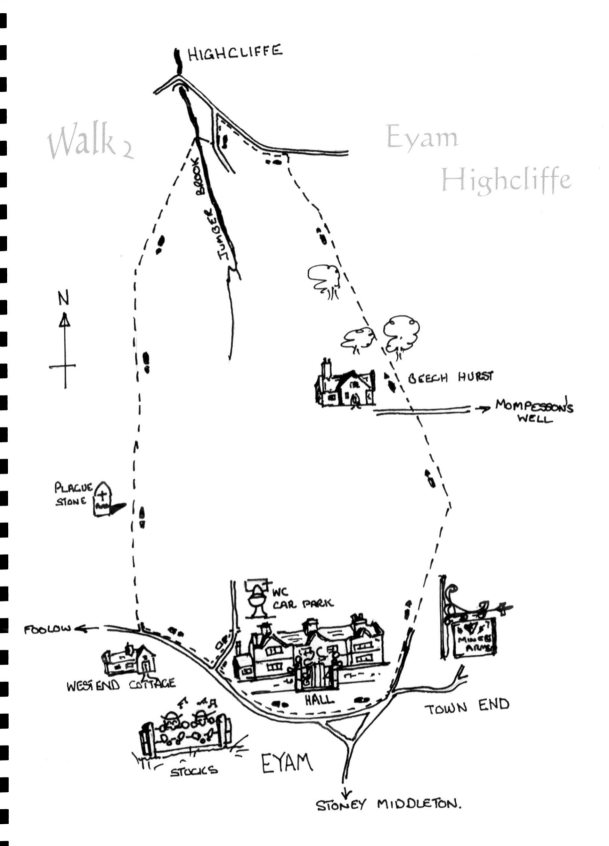

HIGHCLIFFE

Walk 2

Eyam
Highcliffe

JUMBER BROOK

N

BEECH HURST

MOMPESSON'S
WELL

PLAGUE
STONE

WC
CAR PARK

FOOLOW

MINERS
ARMS

WEST END COTTAGE

HALL

TOWN END

STOCKS

EYAM

STONEY MIDDLETON.

Walk 2

Eyam - Highcliffe

About this walk

This is a lovely walk that will probably take just over an hour. Eyam has a fascinating history and you may wish to add some extra time for exploring the village or perhaps consider combining the walk with a visit to the museum, the church or to Eyam Hall. Particular points of interest are listed on page 9.

As you walk above the village you will enjoy beautiful views over Eyam and its surrounding landscape. During the late summer and autumn this walk provides an excellent opportunity for blackberry picking along the route!

Distance	3.3km.
Terrain	A mixture of pavement, lanes, tracks, woodland, fields and footpaths. There is a steepish but gradual ascent from the village up to Highcliffe, but after this stage of the walk, the way is either level or downhill. Some areas can be muddy and a little slippery after rain, but in general the surfaces are good, with only a few short stretches where the going gets slightly rough and uneven.
Map	OS Explorer OL24 The Peak District, White Peak area. 1:25 000 scale.
Starting Point	Eyam car park on Hawkhill Road, off Church Street (pay and display). Church Street is the main street running through Eyam village. Grid reference SK 216 767.
Refreshments	Eyam has several attractive pubs, teashops and cafés offering a range of drinks, snacks and meals.

✓ *Before leaving car park, have a look at information board near the entrance giving a concise history of the village.*

1. From car park entrance, turn *left* into **Hawkhill Road** and walk down to T-junction

2. At T-junction turn *right* and walk up towards **Town Head** (Main Road)

✓ *As you walk along, note on your right-hand side the once Royal Oak Inn (now a private residence), Merrill Cottage and Richard Furness' House (all with interesting information plaques).*

3. After **Richard Furness' House**, walk to **West End Cottage** on the other side of the road

✓ *After viewing West End Cottage, walk a little further on to Town Head Factory, which is of historical interest and also has an information plaque explaining its varied past. After this, the walk resumes from West End Cottage.*

4. After viewing **Town Head Factory**, return to **West End Cottage** and re-cross road

5. Take lane between houses, almost opposite **West End Cottage**

6. Go straight up, through gate and then through further gate at top of lane

7. Head up left hand-side of field towards house opposite and at this house turn *left* to follow path (wall on both sides)

8. As wall ends, turn *right* up pathway in front of house (ignore private drive going down)

9. On reaching field, bear right (keep side of house on right)

10. As you meet wall, turn *left* and head up field (keep wall on right)

11. Carry on up as wall gradually reduces to rubble!

12. Follow path up as it bears slightly right and soon climbs up through a wooded area

13. Go over small wooden stile in fence and follow path as it dips down

14. Cross stream and continue to follow path as it bears right up hill

15. At top of path go through small gate, then turn *left* up lane

16. When lane meets quiet road, turn *right* and walk along road

17. Shortly after passing a bungalow on right (Northlands), ignore footpath on left. A few paces further on, go through small gate on right

18. Cross field diagonally to bottom left-hand corner

19. Go through small gate and follow footpath to edge of wood

20. Go through further small gate and continue (keep wall and wood on right)

21. After going through small gate in opposite wall, turn *right* and follow path down

22. Continue as path bears to left (with wall on right)

23. Path soon leads away from wall and now has a stone slab surface

24. Go through gate, down a few steps, cross road and turn *left*

25. After a few paces go through gate on right and down steps

26. A few paces further on, bear left across field (do not take footpath going straight down)

27. Head for bottom left hand-side of field, go through gate and turn *right*

28. Follow lane down, eventually passing the **Miners Arms** and on to **The Square**

29. On reaching **The Square** turn *right* and head to **Church Street**

✓ **You may like to take refreshment in one of the village cafés (or pubs!) before finishing the walk. See page 9 for points of historic interest in the village.**

30. Follow **Church Street** through village until you reach **Hawkhill Road** on right

31. Turn *right* into **Hawkhill Road** and walk up the hill to return to car park

Interesting points to view on the Stoney Middleton Walk (Walk 3)

Riley Graves - above the village lies a desolate walled enclosure containing the gravestones of the Hancock family, a father, his three sons and three daughters. They were all buried by Mrs Hancock within eight days of each other. (Even several centuries on, it is hard not to be moved when visiting this lonely site.)

Parish Church of St. Martin (Stoney Middleton) - local history asserts that Joan Eyre built the first church of St. Martin in thanksgiving for her husband's safe return from Agincourt in 1415. Original 15th century tower is all that remains of that building. The unusual octagonal nave (one of only two in the country) was added in 1759 after fire, two years earlier, had destroyed everything but the tower.

Roman Baths - believed to be the site of Roman Baths, fed by a thermal spring. There was a Roman settlement in the area, probably based on lead mining.

Toll House - an octagonal building (now a fish and chip shop!) built in 1840 to collect dues from travellers along the new turnpike road passing through Stoney Middleton.

Lover's Leap Café - along the main street in Stoney Middleton, next to the Post Office. This stands on the place where Hannah Baddeley leapt from an eighty-foot cliff in 1762 after being jilted. She was saved by her billowing petticoats, suffering only cuts and bruises, but sadly died two years later aged 26.

Boundary Stone - one of the points where food was left for Eyam villagers during the time of the plague.

Ring a Ring o' Roses

Ring a ring o' roses,
A pocket full of posies,
Atishoo! Atishoo!
We all fall down!

This macabre traditional 'nursery rhyme' is believed by some to have originated in the time of the plague.

The ring of roses probably refers to the pink coloured rash that was one of the first symptoms of the plague.

Posies were the herbs and spices carried to fend off infection and mask the smell

Sneezing was believed to be a sure sign that some one was about to die.

The last line omits the word 'dead' but may refer to the inevitable death that followed the symptoms.

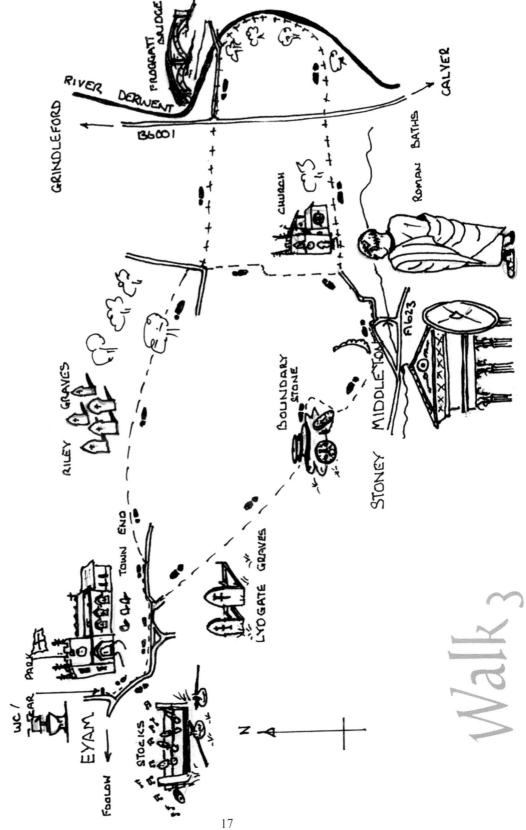

Walk 3

Walk 3

Eyam - Stoney Middleton (With optional extension to the River Derwent)

About this walk

Allow plenty of time for this walk - the village itself includes so many points of historical interest that you may find you take quite a bit longer than anticipated. It is a delightful walk and there are impressive views of the beautiful Peak District countryside from many points. Particular areas of interest, both within the village and along the route, are listed on pages 9 and 16. The walled area of Riley Graves is very poignant, even when viewed nearly three and a half centuries later.

Distance	5.5km (7.5km if you add the optional walk to the riverside).
Terrain	A mixture of lanes, tracks and footpaths. Some areas can be muddy after rain, but in general the surfaces are good. There is a steepish descent into Stoney Middleton and a slightly steep walk up towards the boundary stone.
Map	OS Explorer OL24 The Peak District, White Peak area. 1:25 000 scale.
Starting Point	Eyam car park on Hawkhill Road, off Church Street (pay and display). Church Street is the main street running through Eyam village. Grid reference SK 216 767.
Refreshments	Eyam has several attractive pubs, teashops and cafés offering a range of drinks, snacks and meals. Stoney Middleton offers a fish and chip shop (the old Toll House) in addition to pubs and Lover's Leap café.

✓ **Before leaving car park, have a look at information board near the entrance giving a concise history of the village.**

1. From car park entrance, turn *left* into **Hawkhill Road** and walk down to T-junction

2. At T-junction turn *left* into **Church Street** and follow it through village

3. When you reach **The Square** (where there are a number of cafés and shops) take a short detour to the *left* into **Water Lane** to view **Miners Arms** and information plaque

4. Then return to **The Square**, turn *left* onto **The Causeway** and head up the hill (**Causeway** soon becomes **New Road**)

5. You will see a row of terraced cottages on left called **Burch Place**

6. Shortly after these cottages, bear *left* into Riley Lane

7. Follow lane up hill for about 360m, until you come to a fork in road

8. Bear *right* at fork and continue up lane for approximately 280m, where you will see the wall surrounding **Riley Graves** on your left

9. After viewing graves rejoin lane and continue up hill

10. At private road turn *right* onto path into a wooded area

11. At next junction turn *right* and follow path down the hill

12. When you reach a gate, go through it and continue straight on (keep wall on your left)

✓ **To your left are impressive views of Froggatt, Curbar and Baslow Edges**

13. Where path meets road, go through stile at side of gate

❖ **If you are doing the extension to this walk (River Derwent) go to page 21**

14. Cross road and immediately turn *left*, walk a few paces and then turn sharp *right* (do not take footpath by gateway)

15. Walk down surfaced lane, with two ponds on your left (but ignoring footpath by ponds)

16. Follow lane down the hill, eventually passing a Lych-gate and graveyard on your left, to reach village of **Stoney Middleton**

✓ **A Lych-gate is a roofed gateway of a churchyard where traditionally a coffin awaited the clergyman's arrival.**

17. Keep following road, passing (alleged!) **Roman Baths** on your right and continue along road as it bears left (ignore turn on your left)

✓ **The hill garden to side of building offers fine views and a good rest point**

18. Pass the Parish Church of **St. Martin** on your left and follow road round as it bears right up to T-junction, turn *right* and walk up the hill

✓ **This is one of only two octagonal churches in the country**

19. At next road junction, just before main road, turn *right* up the hill (do not take the road marked **The Fold**) but bear left up road marked **Cliff Bottom**

Riley Grave

✓ **A little way up CLIFF BOTTOM, look down on your left to see the old octagonal TOLL HOUSE which is now a fish and chip shop**

20. Carry on up the hill for approximately 100m, until you see a stile on your left leading to a path up a grassy hill. Cross stile and continue up this path

✓ **Just over the brow of the hill and beyond the trees on the right, note the plague Boundary Stone (no plaque) on your right**

21. Carry on along path to stone wall opposite and go through stile

✓ **On left, behind grassy mound, is a disused lead mine called CLIFF STYLE**

22. Carry on along path, passing through a further stile, gate posts and to the side of 2 large gates (beside houses)

23. On meeting road, carry straight on down (ignore road on your right)

✓ **You will shortly see the Lydgate Graves on your left**

24. When you reach **The Square** cross road and then turn *left* along **Church Street**

25. Follow **Church Street** through village, until you reach **Hawkhill Road** on right

26. Turn **right** into **Hawkhill Road** and walk up the hill to return to car park

Froggatt Bridge

Extension to River Derwent (optional extra to the **Stoney Middleton** walk)

1. Cross road and immediately turn *left* and walk to gate (ignore track to right going down the hill)

2. Go through small gate at side of large one and head down field towards road (keeping wall on your left)

✓ **Below and slightly to your left you can see the village of FROGGATT and FROGGATT EDGE above it**

3. When you reach next gate, go over stile at side and straight down field

4. At opposite end of field, go over stile, cross road and head down lane directly opposite

5. As you reach bridge, cross over stile on your right

6. Go down footpath heading through wooded area, along **River Derwent**

✓ **Notice that the two arches of the bridge are of different shapes and sizes**

7. Go through first stile and walk diagonally across field, up to top right hand corner (keeping river on left)

8. Cross stile in corner of field, just up from gate

9. Turn immediately *right* and head up field towards farm (keeping wall to your right)

10. At top of field go through small gate and cross road. Go up lane beside **Knouchley Farm**

11. As you reach farm house and buildings on left, footpath bears right and passes alongside these buildings (ignore gateway on right)

12. Go through gateway and when you reach edge of farm buildings turn *left* (ignore path going straight on) and walk down side of building to reach field

13. Facing **Calver Village**, bear *right* towards a pair of gates in middle of wall

14. Cross over stile by gate and walk along path (with wall on your right)

15. As path descends a slope and opens out into a meadow, keep on main path leading in direction of village

16. At end of path go through small gate and turn *left* onto surfaced road

❖ **Now rejoin page 19 (THE WALK TO STONEY MIDDLETON) at point 17**

The Grindleford Walks

The incline today

Tollbar Cottage

Padley Mill

Padley Gorge

Letter from the Quarryman

Derwent Valley Water Board
Bole Hill Quarry Site
Nr. Grindleford
Derbyshire

13th February 1903

Dear Ma

Don't drop dead at the shock! This is me, your long lost son, the boy you last set eyes on three years ago - or is it more? Not penned by me, of course. That'd take a bit more schooling than I've had. You're getting this letter thanks to a Mr Pritchard, a gentleman from Wales who's taken me in as one of his lodgers. I'm talking him through it now, him and me sitting at the big table in his living room, a paraffin lamp hanging over us, though he could do with it being a bit brighter. He's found us some decent paper from somewhere - it's not something I often need. And he's been saying for a long time that I should put your mind at rest, before it's too late and perhaps I'll get news that your whole body's been laid down to rest. If that was to happen, so he tells me, I'd never forgive myself. Well maybe I wouldn't, though I'm not one who feels I owe anyone anything. Nothing's ever come to me on a plate. Still, here's hoping this finds you well. You could even try to send me a line back, if you feel the urge to. First time in years I've had something called an address.

Can see you in my mind, going down the street to Aunt Bessie's when you get this, telling her to read it out, that's if she's got any sight left. It'll probably surprise her that I'm not in prison somewhere.

Must be about as far as I've ever been from you, Ma. Up in Derbyshire, near some place called Grindleford, not that it's worth spitting for. Nearest real town is Sheffield, and a good number of men come in every day from there. By *in* I mean to this quarry - that's the work I'm on. But just saying quarry can't tell you what this place is like. I've worked in a couple of others over the last few months, but they were nothing against this one. We're getting stone out of here to build two hulking great dams - they're going to fill up a whole valley a few miles away, the Derwent Valley it's called. It'll take years to build them - which is all to the good as far as I'm concerned - and when they're done they'll hold enough water for half the country, by the sound of it.

Could have worked right there, right on the dams. That's where I first landed up after I walked out of the last job. Took me long enough to get there, just on something I'd heard, not knowing if I was sure of work at the end of it. Couldn't believe my eyes - nothing like any of the dumps I'd worked at before. Usually you're lucky if there's as much as a leaking shed roof over your head. At most places there's men sleeping out in old tents, or else they're under hedges, in hen houses, just about anywhere. Last place I was, one of the older men died in the night. Nothing wrong that you could see, just cold, hungry, living a hard life for too long. Nobody in charge gave a toss. But at these dams there's a proper set up, what you'd call a sort of navvy village. There's rows of houses, a canteen, a few shops, the lot. Even a little hospital! Youngsters all round the place too, and they've got proper schoolrooms for them there. Tin Town, they call the place, because the houses are made of corrugated iron on the outside. Well I knew right away that I'd stay there a while if I got the chance, if nothing else just to get into a proper bed for a bit. They told me I was to sleep over at the doss house for the first night. That's the rule, and if you don't get an offer of work the next day, you've got to move on. That'd have been a big blow. Just as well I'd got enough on me to pay for the night - sixpence it cost me.

It was all right, that doss house - a bed to myself, clean sheets, clean night-shirt. First rule is - you take a bath, and when I was sitting there in it in it, scrubbing myself down, this woman (sort of female you don't argue with) put my clothes in a sack and made off with them. That got me worried! Only had what I'd stood up in. Got them back next morning - stank of disinfectant, but not so much of grime and sweat.

Anyway, there was even a good bit of bacon for breakfast, and then a while later one of the bosses had a word with me. Pricked his ears up when I told him about the quarrying I'd done. Said they needed a few more men up at Bole Hill - that's this place - and would I be willing to work on that end of things? Told me there were huts to lodge in up here, just like the ones I'd already seen. Said to him I wasn't bothered, just so long as I had a bed to lie in and some paid work. And that was that. By the rules, I should have stayed in that doss house for a full week, just in case I was carrying smallpox or something. But he said I looked well enough and he didn't seem to want any hanging around. Told me he could see I had look in my eye, and a mouth on me, and he warned me to keep it shut. Rules were strict, he said, there was to be no answering back, no fighting, no getting drunk. I said I'd manage that, for as long as it suited me. So he got me up here on the train that morning, and I was put on to work next day.

This place looks just like ants swarming over an ant hill - must be around four hundred men - and there's rock faces being worked all over the hillside, and further. They've put down tracks, so engines and wagons can get along the ledges underneath rock faces, and you can see great lifting cranes everywhere, bringing down huge blocks to be put on the wagons. Nearly 30 tons each, those blocks weigh. Mostly I'm working at the foot of a face, helping to get blocks of a crane, knocking rough ends off with a pick, making sure they're good enough for putting into the walls of those two dams. The rock's about as hard as you'll ever get. Gritstone, it's called, and it's a real devil to work on, takes a strong man to do it. Even needs explosives, sometimes, to loosen it out of the rock. And I'm told there's more than two million tons of the stuff here. We get about six thousand tons a week out if there's no hold ups. Thing is, whole lot's got to be pushed three hundred feet down a very steep hill to get it to the main railway line below, that's the railway that takes it off to the dams. There's a great winding drum at the top of the hill, turning a cable, and the trick is that an empty wagon coming up lets a full one go down. Scares you when you first set eyes on it. Operated by a brake-man called Tom Green and I wouldn't mind being put on it if he ever goes, but I don't suppose it's likely to come my way.

Anyway, you're probably not too bothered about all that. Don't know what you're bothered about, Ma, to be truthful, except where the next penny's coming from. Now that I've got myself together a bit, I'll try and send you a pound or two from time to time. Wages aren't bad here - sevenpence ha'penny an hour, though there's a lot that think we should be on at least a penny more. Talk is that we'll be out on strike for it by next month.

Course I have to pay for food, which isn't cheap here, though it's not the swindling price they charge at a lot of sites. And I give Mr P a fair bit for my lodging. There's four of us at the moment sleeping in his lodgers' room, but faces have changed a bit over the months. Rules are too strict here for some, they can't take it, or they can't keep off the drink. Mr and Mrs P have a bedroom, and then there's this living room for the whole lot of us, though we're on our own in here just now. Others are across in one of the mess rooms, playing cards. There's a cooking range in here, I can throw some bacon or something on it and brew a pot of tea, but Mrs P quite often cooks stew and dumplings and then we'll all sit round of an evening. Other huts are nearly all just for working men. It's not families here, not like at Tin Town. Place is always kept clean, though, but they still inspect it once a week to make sure.

We've got no hospital or school at Bole Hill. No children around here, and that's good, because they can get on your nerves. If there's an accident, a doctor comes in from a place called Hathersage - bit bigger than Grindleford but still nothing much. Takes him a while to get here, which isn't funny if it's a bad injury. He had to come up yesterday, as a matter of fact. There was a nasty accident, and to be honest that's what's got me round to writing to you, that and Mr P's nagging. Afternoon, it was, but in fact there'd already been an accident in the morning. It's not as if to this is a bad place to work either, not like a lot of sites where there's men getting injured, or worse, by the day. No end of rules here - machines checked every day, no one allowed to work if they're the worse for drink. It's not a place for anyone soft, that I can tell you, but it's about as safe as you'll get in this way of work.

But early on yesterday, couple of men got injured - pushed down from a rock face by a stone that'd worked loose from a crane. Bit messed up they are - one's had all his ribs crushed - but from what I've heard it could have been worse. Shook me up a bit though - I wasn't far off when they fell - but not nearly so bad as in the afternoon, when I heard what'd happened to Will. Bit daft, Will, bit of a simpleton. Came in from Hathersage every day and he'd been working with me on the same face for a good while. Few years older than me, about middle twenties. Took him under my wing a bit, don't know why. Not often I bother about anyone else, my own fights are more than enough, I don't choose to take on other people's. But for some reason I kept an eye out for Will, made sure the others didn't yell at him too much for being slow, gave him a hand now and then. Anyway yesterday afternoon he wasn't up on the face with me, he was at the bottom of the slope, though I still don't know why. Three wagons broke loose from the cable halfway up the hill and went crashing down the line. A lot of us heard yelling and shouting from down there, but then there's always a lot of noise around. Will was a bit deaf, but maybe if he'd been brighter he'd have got away in time. Hit full on, he was, flesh and blood all over the lines. No point in getting Dr Lander out, nothing anyone could do for him. He's been taken off to lie at the Millstone Inn just down the road, what was still in one piece that is, and there's going to be some fuss about it because it should never have happened. Upset a lot of men, it did, even though they'd seen a good many accidents in their time. That's why Mr P said it would do me good to write this letter to you.

Anyway Ma, Mr P's looking tired now. It's taken us a few hours to pen this, and that's after we've done a full day's labour. He's good to do this for me, can't ever remember anyone taking trouble for me like he does. Almost like having a dad, not that I'd know. It'll be a while before you're likely to see me at the door again, though I don't fool myself that me being a long way off gives you much grief. Going to stay here as long as it lasts, or at least as long as I can hold that temper of mine in and not land myself in trouble. Better chance of that now than there was before. I might even keep my eyes open for a girl up here.

You'd be surprised if you saw me - don't look at all bad when I'm scrubbed up and I'm not short of a bit of muscle. A lot of girls like that, especially if you've got a bob or two to spend on them. First time I've ever had a bit to spare. There's a few of the men taken up with local girls. Had their fill of moving all over the country, from one dump to another.

Can't think what on earth this place will look like when we're through with the stone, when it's all packed up and we're gone. Won't be for a long while of course. Whole hill's been torn apart, you can't think that anything green will ever grow on it again. Not that it worries me, plenty of other hills around here.

Look after yourself, Ma.

Yours ever, *Frank*

Looking up the railway incline toward Bole Hill Quarry from near to the siding to the immediate west of Grindleford Station. A wagon load of large stones is descending and is at the same time hauling the distant empty wagon up the hill, via the cable passing over the winding drum. The speed of the connected wagons was controlled by Tom Green who operated the brake on the drum. At the upper right can be seen parts of some of the bungalows that were erected for those workmen at the site who required housing. The course of the incline, the lower end of which now passes beneath the lane at Upper Padley (SK 246790), can still be readily located, as can the remains of the foundations of the bungalows.

Walk 4

SHEEPFOLD

HATHERSAGE MOOR

CARL WARK

QUARRIES

HATHERSAGE

MILLSTONE EDGE

BURBAGE BRIDGE

A625

B6521

BURBAGE BROOK

LONGSHAW LODGE

N

BOLEHILL

LONGSHAW ESTATE

GRINDLEFORD STATION

Grindleford
Bole Hill
Carl Wark
Longshaw Lodge

CAR PARK

TUNNEL

PADLEY

GRINDLEFORD

27

Walk 4

Grindleford - Bole Hill - Carl Wark - Longshaw Lodge

About this walk

A really super walk of immense variation, both in historic, archaeological interest and the nature of the countryside. Bole Hill Quarry was used as the source of gritstone for the Howden and Derwent Dams. Carl Wark is thought to have been an Iron Age hill fort. Longshaw Estate was once the shooting lodge of the Dukes of Rutland, and later a convalescent hospital for injured soldiers of the First World War. It is now a National Trust Estate with visitor centre and café.

Distance	8.5km.
Terrain	Early on in the walk (Bole Hill Quarry) some paths are rough underfoot and fairly steep over very short distances. In places, especially around Carl Wark, paths become less distinct but our directions and the visible points to which you are heading will keep you on track! May be muddy or boggy in places and final descent through wood can be a bit slippery after heavy rain.
Map	OS Explorer OL24 The Peak District, White Peak area. 1:25 000 scale.
Starting Point	Parking on approach road to Grindleford station off B6521. Grid reference SK 249 784.
Refreshments	Cafés at Longshaw Lodge and Grindleford Station. After many enjoyable visits, we would especially recommend the café at Longshaw. Open daily from June - September. Limited opening times in winter (Ring 01433 631708 for times). Christmas trees are also sold throughout December!

1. Walk down approach road to station and over railway bridge, passing railway station on left (if you are coming out of station itself, turn left)

2. Continue along (ignore footpath leading into Padley Gorge on right)

3. Shortly after **Padley Mill**, turn *right* and walk up lane

4. At top of lane, go through a gate into **Padley Gorge** and up path for a short distance

5. On reaching a building (with curved roof) on left (valve house), turn *left* in front of building, go straight past double doors, and continue up the path

6. Go through a gate and continue up the hill

7. After a couple of minutes, you will see a stone wall on left (about 20 metres off path). Keep to the path but almost immediately after seeing wall, as path crosses another, turn *left* and follow new path

✓ *This path may be wide and grassy if you walk in the winter or spring, very narrow in summer or early autumn due to bracken growth*

8. As path opens out, the remains of a stone structure can be seen (base for winding drum)

✓ **The flat surface of this, and other paths round here, were the working areas of the quarries. Gritstone was extracted for the construction of the Howden and Derwent dams, and engines and their wagons ran on rails here.**

✓ **The stone structure is the remains of a winding drum which controlled wagons moving up and down rails on the steep incline in front. At the bottom of the incline lay the main railway line along which the stone was transported to the dams. Worth looking down the incline!**

9. Now return along same path and on meeting original upward path, turn *left* and continue up the hill

10. On coming to another small plateau, continue to follow path up a small incline

11. At top of incline follow path as it turns right and up for roughly 60 steps, then turn *left* up a short fairly steep rocky path

12. Continue to follow path as it bears gradually right, up towards trees

13. As path reaches top of hill (quarry face to right) continue along wide flat grassy track

✓ **A large number of ants and anthills can generally be seen in this area - Silver Birch is their favoured tree.**

14. Keep to wide main track (ignore any small paths veering off)

✓ **Many abandoned millstones can be seen on right (these belong to National Trust).**

15. When track eventually meets road, go through a little gate, cross road and take stony footpath directly opposite, leading into a wooded area (ignore path just down to left)

The winding drum at the top of the incline which drops away to the photographer's left. The cutting – seen half left – carries the standard gauge railway out of Bole Hill Quarry to the incline. The drum's stone supporting structure can still be located at the site and a walk around the quarry site (SK 248794), now owned by the National Trust, is of interest and well worthwhile, with many large stones that were quarried but not ultimately used being readily identified by the indentations that had been used in their gripping by the "stone dogs" (callipers pulled tight by a load on a chain during lifting).

Photograph and caption - by kind permission of Prof. Brian Robinson

Millstones

16. Shortly after, as path opens into a wider stony surfaced area, go straight on

17. Continue along main path as it gradually winds along (ignore any turns off this path)

✓ **You will pass a number of ruined buildings and foundations, all of which were part of 'Grey Millstone Quarries'.**

18. Follow path as it bears right between 2 large rocks

19. A few steps beyond these rocks, turn left and follow narrow path to stile (do not continue up the hill)

20. Cross stile (ignore path on left leading to Littlemoor) and follow path across moorland

✓ **The rocks on the right are called Over Owler Tor.**

21. As path meets another one going across, turn left onto it and continue across moorland

✓ **Stanage Edge is ahead and slightly to the left and on many fine days hang gliders can be seen.**

22. Keep on path, ignore turn to right leading up to rocks

23. Eventually, as path winds round to right, the large rocky face of **Higger Tor** will come into view. Follow path round until wall is seen on right (**Higger Tor** now on left)

✓ **Higger Tor is thought to be a Viking burial ground. The name is probably a corruption of the name of a Viking god.**

24. Head for corner of wall on right (sheepfold) and go down side of wall (keeping wall on right)

25. At next corner follow path straight on (this can be indistinct but keep in mind that the point you eventually want to be at is roughly half way between **Higger Tor** on left and **Carl Wark** on right)

26. Keep following path. It later heads up towards **Higger Tor**, but before it does, turn onto path going right (which can be unclear at times). This path heads towards that halfway point (avoid straying too far to the right as the land can get boggy)

✓ **A British tribe known as the Brigantes is thought to have built a hill fort around 100BC. The Vikings later called this Carl Wark, meaning warrior (Carl) and building (Wark).**

27. When path meets main track between **Higger Tor** and **Carl Wark** turn *right* and walk a short distance

❖ **If you wish to explore Carl Wark then carry on along this path. Then return here and continue from point 29.**

28. Turn *left* down path which runs alongside **Carl Wark** (now on your right)

29. Follow path down (it splits to form several paths, any of which you can follow). You are heading for the right hand corner of the large distant wood opposite

30. At the bottom of hill cross stone bridge and head straight up path (keep wood on left)

31. Shortly after, cross a small stream, go up some earthen steps and turn immediately *right* to follow path just above river

32. Continue along path as it eventually bears left away from river

33. In front of a boulder strewn hill, join main path and turn *right*

34. Go through a pair of stone gate posts and then 2 more gates to meet road

35. Cross road, go through gate and straight on (ignore paths going down on right)

36. Bear left as this joins main path and continue up

37. Go through a gate, turn *right* and cross road into driveway by gatehouse. Walk along drive to reach **Longshaw Lodge**

✓ **At Longshaw Lodge there is a National Trust shop, information point, and a very good café serving snacks and meals. Good toilet facilities here.**

38. On leaving café, go straight down towards gate opposite, turn *left* and walk along path

39. Go through gate, turn *right* past engraved millstone and follow path with 'Ha Ha' on left

✓ **A Ha Ha is a concealed wall, constructed in this way so that the view from the house is not spoilt by a visible fence or wall.**

40. Follow this path round, through a number of small gates, to a large pond

41. Just past pond, but before gateway and barn in field on right, turn *left* along a rough track going through a wood (this can be churned up and muddy)

42. At edge of wooded area, follow track as it bears left (meeting another track) and carry on along this track

43. Further on, cross stream and immediately go straight ahead (original track will continue to bear up to the left)

44. After a few paces bear right (by edge of trees) and follow path

45. Cross another stream over small stony bridge and continue

46. Further on, go through gate into woodland and follow path along and eventually down (ignore any paths going off)

47. Where path eventually meets another, carry on down to road, cross road and turn *left*

48. A few paces later, at the end of wall, turn sharp *right* and follow path and then steps to return to start of the walk

Photograph – by kind permission of Captain Murray Clifford C/O National Trust Longshaw Estate

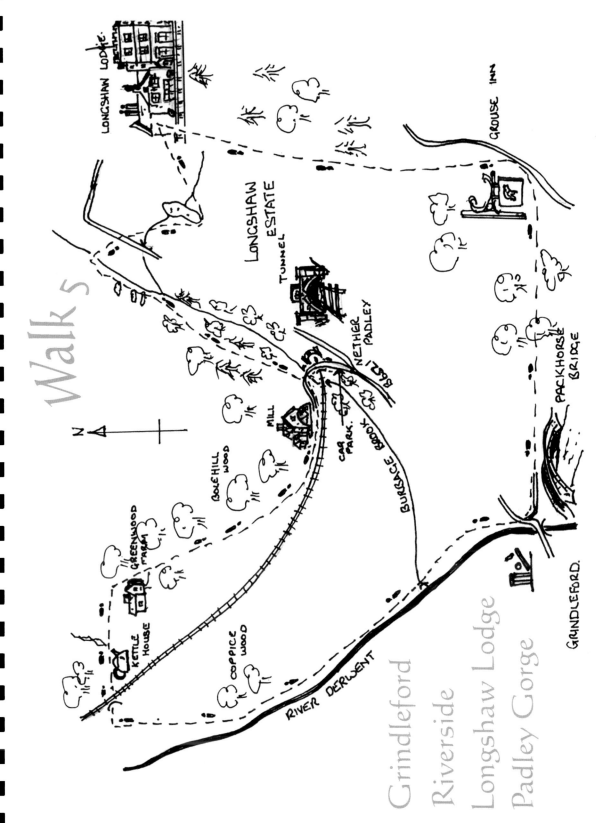

Walk 5

Grindleford
Riverside
Longshaw Lodge
Padley Gorge

33

Walk 5

Grindleford - Riverside - Longshaw Lodge - Padley Gorge

About this walk

A really lovely walk encompassing riverside, attractive woodland, National Trust Estate and the popular Padley Gorge. Lots of historic and archaeological features, with interesting and varied flora.

Distance	12km.
Terrain	A fairly easy walk in that the only significant climb is a steady one through Hay Wood. Some areas can be muddy after rain but the surface is reasonably good underfoot.
Map	OS Explorer OL24 The Peak District, White Peak area. 1:25 000 scale.
Starting Point	Parking on approach road to Grindleford station, off B6521. Grid reference SK 249 784.
Refreshments	Cafés at Longshaw Lodge and Grindleford Station. After many enjoyable visits, we would especially recommend the café at Longshaw. Open daily from June - September. Limited opening times in winter (Ring 01433 631708 for times). Christmas trees are also sold throughout December!

1. Walk down approach road to station and over railway bridge, passing railway station on left (if you are coming out of station itself, turn *left*)

2. Continue along lane (ignore footpath leading into **Padley Gorge** on right)

3. Walk past **Padley Mill** (ignore right turn shortly after this) and continue up lane

✓ *After a while, to your left, is Brunts Barn, Peak National Park Ranger Service Briefing Centre. On your right is Padley Chapel, only remaining part of Padley Hall, famous for 'Padley Martyrs'. Two Catholic priests were arrested there in July 1558 during a raid, found guilty of high treason and condemned to death by hanging, drawing and quartering.*

4. Go straight on over cattle grid into **Longshaw Estate** (ignore next turning on left)

5. Continue up lane, past the end of houses on left and carry on up track

6. When wall on right ends, turn *left* and head down towards wood, then continue on path through wood (wall on right)

7. When path reaches a gate, do **NOT** go through it to cross the railway bridge, but turn *right* and go along grassy path (there is a wall on either side)

8. As path meets wall, go through gate in wall and carry on through wood (railway is on your left)

9. Continue on path as it winds along, crossing a number of streams (ignore gate on right near end of wood)

10. Eventually, at end of wood, go through a small gate and past farm on left

11. Cross farm track and continue straight down

12. Follow path as it bears left, go through a gate and under railway bridge

13. Path then turns *right* and leads over a little stone bridge (a stone water tunnel on right)

14. On reaching stone wall ahead, turn *left* and continue down (with wall on right)

15. When path reaches a surfaced drive turn *left*

16. At cattle grid turn *right* and go through gate

17. Follow grassy path, marked occasionally by large boulders, and continue along as it follows river

18. After a while, go through gate into **Coppice Wood** and continue along path

19. Just after path crosses a small stream, ignore paths on left (to **Grindleford Station**) and continue alongside river. (If the blisters are bad you can always make your escape back to the car from here!)

20. Go through little gate to leave **Coppice Wood** and carry on across field by river

21. Pass through next gate, and then through further gateway (or stile)

22. Very shortly after this, go through gate, over a small bridge and continue along path (keeping wall on left)

23. Walk through stone gateposts, carry along riverside and through gate in corner of field

24. Cross over road in front of church and turn *right*

25. Within short distance, immediately after churchyard gates, turn *left* and walk up lane

✓ Just by ancient packhorse bridge, notice the old Toll Cottage on right.

26. Approximately 300m further up lane, just before house, follow lane through gateway as it bears left into wooded area

27. Shortly after, go through gate into **Hay Wood** and keep wall on left as path rises uphill

28. When wall on left ends, carry straight on uphill (ignore path going left)

29. Path eventually crosses another (a metal cover can be seen in ground at this point). Carry straight on up the hill (ignore any paths going off)

30. Near top of hill, where path joins another, turn *right* and continue up the hill

31. Leave **Hay Wood** through gate (by electricity poles) turn *left* up path towards car park

32. Follow path into car park, turn *left* and continue (ignore car park entrance on right)

33. Approximately 60m from corner of wall, cross stile in wall on right (**Grouse Inn** can be seen in distance)

34. Cross fields diagonally in direction of **Grouse Inn**

35. Go over stile leading to road, and turn *left* past **Grouse Inn** along grass verge (ignore stile on left after about 200m)

36. A little further on, go through a gate (slightly off grass verge on left) marked **Longshaw Estate** (track leads you to **Longshaw Lodge**, approximately 2km away)

37. Walk along this track (passing through a further gate on way)

38. At end of track (where a private area begins) go through 2 small gates and follow path to Lodge

✓ At Longshaw Lodge, there is a National Trust shop, information point, and a very good café serving snacks and meals. Good toilet facilities here.

39. Coming out of visitor centre, head straight back down and follow path left (retracing your steps back to small gate)

40. Go through gate, turn *right* past engraved millstone and follow path with 'Ha Ha' on left

✓ A Ha Ha is a concealed wall, constructed in this way so that the view from the house is not spoilt by a visible fence or wall

41. Follow this path round, through a number of small gates, past a large pond, to road

✓ As the path turns away from the pond, Carl Wark (thought to be an Iron age Fort) and Higger Tor (a Viking burial site) can be seen on the right in the distance.

42. On reaching gate by road, cross over road and turn *right*

43. After a few paces, go through a gap in wall on left and down steps

44. Follow main path down to footbridge and cross stream

45. Turn *left* and take lower path closer to river

46. Follow boulder-strewn path, go through a gate and carry on downhill

✓ This is an 'Ancient Woodland'. To be so called, an area has to be continuous woodland from at least the year 1600.

47. At bottom of a rocky slope, keep to main path (do not take path down to stream's edge, which is very steep)

48. Carry on as path starts to go up hill (ignore path on left that turns back and leads down to stream) and after short time go past a building on right (valve house)

49. Go through a small gate and follow private road down the hill

50. At bottom of road turn *left* and walk past **Padley Mill**. Continue over bridge and back to starting point of walk

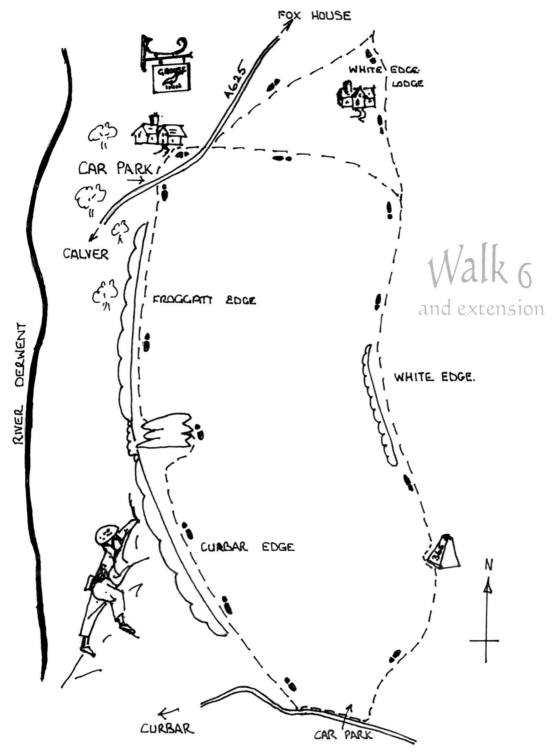

FOX HOUSE

A625

GEORGE

WHITE EDGE LODGE

CAR PARK

CALVER

Walk 6
and extension

FROGGATT EDGE

WHITE EDGE

RIVER DERWENT

CURBAR EDGE

N

CURBAR

CAR PARK

Hay Wood car park - Froggatt
Curbar and White Edges

Walk 6

Hay Wood (car park) - Froggatt Edge - Curbar Edge - White Edge
(with optional extension)

About this walk

An easy to follow route taking in the truly stunning views from the Edges - best on a clear day!

Distance	9km (10.5km if you add the optional walk to the riverside).
Terrain	A mainly flat, but at times a rocky and uneven walk. It includes a number of potentially muddy parts and some short, but steepish, ascents.
Map	OS Explorer OL24 The Peak District, White Peak area. 1:25 000 scale.
Starting Point	Hay Wood National Trust Car Park (pay and display). This car park is on the left just before the Grouse Inn as you head up from Calver or Froggatt on the A625. Grid Reference SK 255 777.
Refreshments	Grouse Inn is at the end of the walk, but you may choose to take your own refreshments. Longshaw Estate is a short drive further up the A625.

1. Go to end of car park (furthest point from entrance) and take footpath leading out of car park, down hill and slightly to left

2. As path descends steeply, go down and through a gap in wall, cross over stream and follow path up opposite side

3. Go through gate, turn *right*, walk a few paces, cross road and walk towards gate

4. Go through entrance by gate and follow wide distinct track as it curves up

5. Continue along for some distance, then pass through a small gate by a large one

6. Keep walking along main wide distinct track (eventually it leads to **Froggatt** and **Curbar Edges**). Ignore any paths off this track

7. As main path forks, just in front of some high rocks, take rocky path going ahead

✓ **After this point the paths run parallel. It is therefore possible to walk either fairly close to the edge or a little further in.**

8. At end of track, drop down to gate to leave **Curbar Edge** and follow footpath towards car park (keeping wall on left)

9. Just before path goes left near corner of wall, turn *right* down steps into **Curbar car park**

10. Head to car park entrance, face the road, and go through gate that is on left from that position

11. Head down track and follow it round (keeping wall on left)

12. At corner of wall, where track forks, keep going straight on and down

13. Where path passes close to a wall, continue straight on down and keep wall on left (ignore gate)

14. Follow path as it dips towards a wooden bridge and then rises again

15. As path nears top of hill, follow it to left, keeping wall on left (ignore path to right)

16. Continue on main path, which will head up and along **White Edge**, passing near a triangulation point (small concrete pillar with metal strips inserted in top) on right

17. Continue along path and *eventually*, on approaching a wall ahead, note **Grouse Inn** beside road on left

18. Go through gap in wall and turn *left* (ignore path going straight on to **Longshaw**)

❖ **If you wish to do the extension walk, do not turn left, carry straight on and follow the instructions given in the extension walk on page 40.**

19. Follow path down (keep wall on left)

✓ **The Grouse Inn is now more visible down and to the left.**

20. As path drops down a rocky stretch, continue downhill into a wooded area (ignore path going right)

21. Go through a gate, turn *right* and head down field towards Inn

22. Go through another gate, turn *left*, walk a few paces and cross over road

23. In front of Inn, walk approximately 30 metres (about 42 steps) downhill and go over a stile on right

24. Follow path across field towards trees opposite, passing between stone gateposts in middle of field and head diagonally left (over remains of wall) to stile in wall

25. Cross over stile, turn *left* and take path going down (with wall on left) back to car park

Mother's Cap

The Optional Extension to White Edge Lodge (NT holiday cottage)
(These instructions will take you back to the start of the walk)

1. Go through gap in wall and carry straight on, follow path across open moorland

2. Eventually go through a gate on left (ignore paths on right)

3. Follow path down to house **(White Edge Lodge)**

✓ **Lodge is owned by the National Trust and let out as a holiday property.**

4. Turn *left* as you reach house (keeping boundary wall of house on your right)

5. At corner of this wall follow path diagonally across open land

6. Just under half way between house and road, bear left as path joins a track and continue downhill towards road

7. Go through a gate, turn *left* and after a few paces cross road

8. Continue to walk on grass verge down road until **Grouse Inn** is reached

9. In front of Inn, walk approximately 30 metres (about 42 steps) downhill and go over a stile on right

10. Follow path across field towards trees opposite, passing between stones gateposts in middle of the field

11. Cross over stile, turn *left* and take path going down (with wall on left) back to car park

Ashford in the Water Walks

Sheepwash Bridge

Ashford Church   *Village Pump*   *Wooden Seat*

The Marble Man's Tale

The candle's not got long to go now. It was a nasty thing, giving off the evil smell of pig tallow. The air in the shed is stuffy, but cold. I shall be glad enough to get inside the house, have some beer and a plate of hot stew. Working days have been long of late, longer than ever.

"This stuff needs to be good," so the man in Matlock Bath has told me. "It must be of the very best" he says, "if I'm to take it to London for that exhibition in the Crystal Palace." Well, I pride myself that my work is as good as any in Ashford - why else would he keep buying bits from me, to sell in what he calls his museum? But if it's taken to London, then who knows? Please God it might put more meat on the table, even give us a little to put by in case times get harder.

Alice should have got the young ones to bed by now - six of them, if you count James, though at twelve he's not really young any more. Of course they won't be asleep, there'll be a din going on in that room up there, and I'll be expected to bellow up the staircase and make sure it stops - or else. Can't blame them, but you've got to be hard with children or they'll run all over you. Alice is heavy and exhausted, she hasn't been well from the start this time, in fact the sooner it's born the better. And if I could have my wish, then this would be the last one. There's plenty of folk around with more, but seven hungry bellies are enough for me, and enough for Alice, what with the one she lost a few years back. Of course it'll be eight in all, but Claire went into service earlier this year when she reached fourteen, up at Thornbridge Hall, and very lucky she was to be taken in there. Not many village girls get such a chance, but then Clara is more polite and tidier looking than most. She wasn't too happy about going, and nor was Alice, but I was firm. "She'll get three decent meals a day there," I said, "and the chance to learn some respectable ways. She might even marry something a bit better than what you see around the village." And of course, it's one less mouth to feed.

Don't misunderstand me, the children get as much food as there is going. There's many a time I've taken less than I had the appetite for, so they wouldn't go hungry. Since my sister Sarah lost her two eldest, I suppose I've had an even greater care for my own. Two healthy strong boys, eight and ten years they were, fell down an old mineshaft a few months back while out larking around. Bodies not found for days on end. You can imagine what it was like. She even lost the one she was carrying, in all that grief. The whole village was out for the funerals of course, as it usually is. There's some that want to grieve with you, there's some that want to pray it won't happen to them, and there's some that just enjoy the spectacle - whether it's of joy or grief. They weren't the first to be killed by falling down a shaft, far from it. There's been more than a small number over the last few years, and not just around this village either. Those hills are death traps, it's time that something was done to stop it. It's surely not impossible to cover the damn holes up! But then, it's not the children of the rich getting killed, is it? They're not left out to roam around, are they? Couldn't keep mine shut up inside - we'd all go mad, or else I'd probably kill them. One living room, that's what we have, the one with the range. There's a little front room, but

Alice makes sure that's kept nice for Sundays, and then only for her and myself, and the odd visitor. Otherwise it wouldn't be nice for long, would it? It's her one pride and joy, that room, especially the corner cabinet with a couple of bits of china her mother passed on to her when we got married. Fifteen years ago that, spring of 1836. We didn't marry until she was pregnant with Clara. That might surprise you, but lots of country folk don't marry until there's the first on its way. It's easier for a single girl to get proper work, and it's best to hold on to that for as long as you can. Alice used to work a stocking frame up the village - four or five lasses in a workshop upstairs. Mind you, there wasn't much future left in it. It went years ago, all that kind of trade has moved to bigger places now, into factories nearer the towns.

Alice's older sister even suggested she should get rid of the baby. "You're only eighteen," she said, "you've plenty of time yet," and offered to get her a tot of turpentine. Alice didn't drink it though. She was already living with me here, it was my father's cottage then, and she knew I'd marry her. Just as well I did, because she nursed him through that terrible time before he died, weaker than a new born babe, not able to raise a spoon to his mouth or put one shaking foot to the floor. That's thirty years of lead mining for you. He was forty-five years old and he'd had a longer life than a good many of those that worked alongside him.

Of course, I should have been a miner myself. The family hasn't known much else other than its menfolk working the mines. Three older brothers were at the Magpie, out near Sheldon, a wretched place, always flooding. The eldest was drowned down there, and the place has lost many a miner that way or crushed under falling rocks. There's some folk believe there must be a curse on that place. Of course lead mining's on the wane now and there's plenty of men out of work, lots of children not getting the food they need. The Magpie's even had to close at times, and then the two of them have been out looking for something else. William wanted to join up with me a while back. "We could make this business bigger," he says, "build a proper workshop, make more stuff, sell it all ourselves." He thinks that black marble's here to stay, that the price will keep going up.

The trouble is, William just hasn't got the skill in his hands, never could have. After all the years of rough work he's done, his hands are like great red shovels. I doubt if there's an ounce of sensitive flesh in his fingertips. If you pushed a pin into them I'd be surprised if he so much as noticed it. It's just not a skill he could be taught, and in any case those huge hands would never be steady enough, because like most miners he's very fond of his beer. They say it protects them from being poisoned by the lead, that's what I'm often told, but I've got my doubts. In any case I'm someone who likes to work on my own. The shed's small, you can barely call it a workshop, but when I'm in here chipping away at the marble, forming the white jasmine flowers that I've made a bit of a speciality of, I'm my own man and I'm answerable to no one else.

Of course it's not really marble, its limestone of a type you can polish up until it's jet black, smooth and gleaming, like nothing else you'll ever see. His Grace the Duke at Chatsworth has got a good bit of it around his house, and the Queen herself bought a table of it a few years back. Of recent times it's the pretty designs inlaid in it that make black marble so special, the flowers, the leaves. Those of us with the skill to do it often favour a particular bloom, and we pride ourselves in creating a true representation, as well as a beautiful one. When I look at the white flowers of my jasmine, the bend of the green leaves, all laid into the shining black surface as if they'd been formed there, I get a real pride. Rub your finger over the surface and you feel no join, no line, nothing. That's the real skill, you see, but it takes years to perfect, and the doing of it is hard and painstaking. Most days I've a badly aching back from sitting on this stool, a brooch or a small vase or some such article held between my knees, bending over it for hours on end. Those of us that earn our living this way are often called 'baublers', an insult if ever there was one. The things we make are of great beauty, trinkets or baubles they are most certainly not. Trinkets cost a lot less for a start. I gave a little brooch to Clara when she went up to the hall, just a simple oval thing with a tiny white flower. She wears it for church and it's already been much admired, so I gather. There may even be an order or two coming from up there, I certainly hope so.

I have to make small things here, there isn't the space for doing tables and the like. And anyway I wouldn't want to put all my efforts for too long into one large object. It might make a lot more money, but if things go wrong towards the end, it's a lot more lost, isn't it? I couldn't afford to contemplate that. So I keep to brooches and pendants and small plates and vases. Sometimes visitors to the village buy from our door - I always keep a few bits in the window of the front room. And of course occasionally the man with the museum in Matlock Bath comes and buys quite a few objects, and orders yet more. He sells a lot in his museum, it's a shop by another name, where people who come up to take the spa waters can wander around and admire. He buys from all over the place, so he tells me, as far as Buxton and Derby. But he certainly seems to like what I do here, and if I did as William has suggested, expand things, perhaps take a lad on to train, then maybe I'd make a fair bit more. But as I said, I like my own company, I don't want to be at anyone's beck and call, and my needs are few. The children are fed well enough, mainly on Alice's turnip and onion stew, which she seems to have simmering most of the day on the range, stocked up from the supply of vegetables under our bed. There's nowhere else to keep them and anyway it's dark under there and fewer mice around than downstairs. I like stew best when there's some pork in it, and there sometimes is on account of the old sow we keep out in the back. She's been a good breeder, it's worth paying the farmer for the use of his boar occasionally. Teaches the young ones a bit about life at the same time, because those beasts don't exactly go about things quietly. It was an eye opener to me as a young lad, and it saved my father, who wouldn't have known what words to say to me, from ever having to open his mouth. Saves me the same thing, and there's no better teacher than nature.

Of course there's not a lot left over from our plates to feed the sow on. The children learnt early on that if they don't eat what's on the table, then there's nothing else. But she gets the scrapings of the pot, as well as peelings and any windfall crabby apples or acorns that the children can find. Anyway she seems to produce good young that fatten up well. It's the fat you want of course, it sticks to the chest much better than lean, especially in winter.

I like beer with a meal if there's any going, though I don't personally frequent the village alehouses - rough places they are, often open till the early hours of the morning. Alice sometimes makes a good beer, a tasty one but not strong, though it once proved too strong when we used to store it in the children's bedroom. James and Robert took a deal too much one evening, and spilt as big a quantity as they drank. Then they were up and down to the back all night long and half the next day. I didn't take the belt to them until they were recovered, and then not too hard. There's plenty of fathers would have taken it to them there and then and who wouldn't have spared it. I didn't let them mess up the privy though - that's really just for me and Alice, though James is now allowed to use it so long as he keeps it clean. The younger ones use the dug up bit of ground beyond the yard.

It's a hard life keeping them fed, trying to keep them clean, bringing them up with some decent Christian ways. Maybe I'll see if the boys can show any skill at this trade, and try to encourage them in it. My three boys can read better than I know how to, even George, who's only just seven. We're luckier than most villages, in that there is a free school for them, though James won't be going there for a great deal longer. Even the girls can get some learning at their cottage school, though Alice can't always spare Mary, the nine-year-old. She's the only girl old enough to be of help in the house, and there are times when there's more work to do than one pair of hands can manage. But then, learning's not too important for girls. Alice can barely read and yet she's a very capable wife.

The only worry I have is this - when I look at the stuff I make, these small things we live off, I often think - what happens if the fashions change? There's a good few of us around here making these things, a lot of families relying on the trade, and there's not much else for us if rich people decide they don't want to buy it anymore. I don't think that will happen, but then you can never tell. People are fickle, especially women.

The candle's in its last flickering moments now. I'll pinch the damn thing out and go inside. It'll be warm in that room and I'll eat with Alice and then get her to rest. There are always clothes to be made, clothes to mend, her days are even longer than mine. And I wouldn't swap with her either, this shed is a haven, rough though it is. The children know never to disturb me here, they know better than to make so much as a sound outside this door. Alice has got the little ones under her feet all day, and she frets about putting enough food on the table to feed bellies, about finding enough cloth to make decent garments to put them in. Still, women were intended to have children and to care for them, it's nature's way. Just as it's my task to provide the means.

Enjoy your walk around our village. It's a prettier, cleaner place now. There are a few more houses of course, though far fewer people. That tells you something! The hills around are fine and glorious, though I never walked them much myself. Never had the time. They've covered most of the shafts for you now, so there shouldn't be any danger there. But of course the ways are steep and rough.

Take care, and God bless.

Inlaid 'Black Marble' Tabletop

45

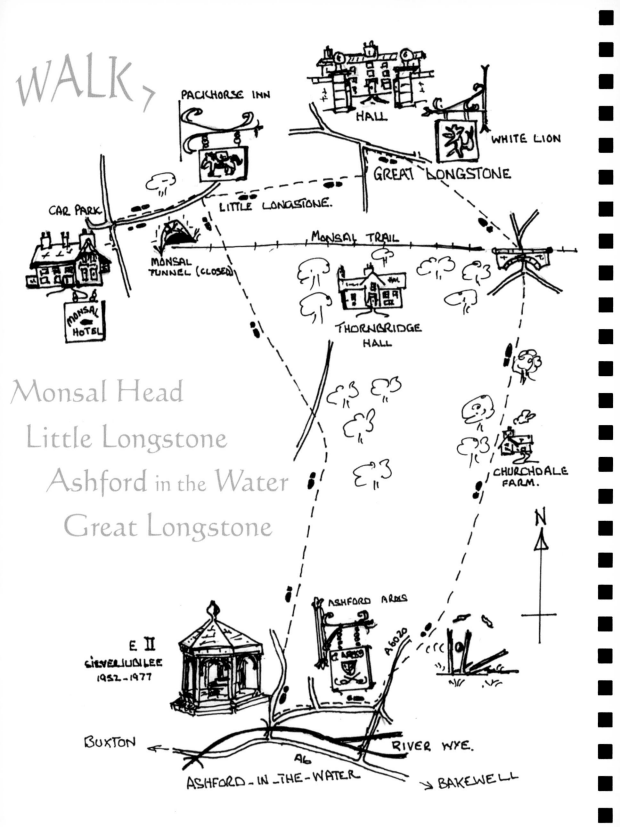

WALK 7

PACKHORSE INN

HALL

WHITE LION

GREAT LONGSTONE

CAR PARK

LITTLE LONGSTONE.

MONSAL TRAIL

MONSAL HOTEL

MONSAL TUNNEL (CLOSED)

THORNBRIDGE HALL

CHURCHDALE FARM.

Monsal Head
Little Longstone
Ashford in the Water
Great Longstone

N

E II
SILVER JUBILEE
1952 - 1977

ASHFORD ARMS

A6020

BUXTON

RIVER WYE.

A6

ASHFORD - IN - THE - WATER

BAKEWELL

Walk 7

Monsal Head - Little Longstone - Ashford in the Water - Gt. Longstone

About this walk

This walk starts at Monsal Head with its spectacular views over Monsal Dale. From that point it becomes a true 'village walk'. You will pass through three very attractive, typically English villages, separated by lovely and varied countryside. Easy two hour walk with plenty of watering holes!

Distance	8km.
Terrain	Not a challenging walk, but a gentle amble through a mixture of villages, paths, trails and fields.
Map	OS Explorer OL24 The Peak District, White Peak area. 1:25 000 scale.
Starting Point	Car park situated at Monsal Head, beside the Monsal Head Hotel on the B6465 (pay and display). Grid reference SK 185 715.
Refreshments	Ashford in the Water offers pubs and a teashop with limited opening hours. At Monsal Head there is a café and hotel. In summer there is generally an ice cream van at this point. You will pass pubs offering meals in each village and Ashford and Great Longstone have local shops.

✓ *Before starting walk, do go to viewpoint, accessed from rear of car park.*

1. From car park entrance turn *left* and immediately *right* in front of hotel, into **Little Longstone**. Go past **Packhorse Inn** on left

2. At end of village, past **'The Hollow'** B&B on right and farm on left, turn *right* through gate or stile and straight on towards **Ashford** and **Monsal Trail** (ignore path to left)

3. Go through small gate and continue ahead, then further small gate and carry on up (wall on right)

4. Shortly after, go over stile on right, which joins the **Monsal Trail**

5. Turn *left*, after a few paces turn *right* down steps, head for stile in opposite wall (next to wooded area)

6. Go over stile, turn *left* and continue, passing through 2 further stiles and 2 small gates

7. Go through further stile, cross lane and through stile on opposite side

8. After a gate, go straight on (farm on right) through further gate then downhill through stile in wall (by a small building)

9. Go up stony track to road, cross road diagonally and go through gate on other side

10. Cross field and go through stile in wall, turn *left* to go along road and carry on down (ignore any side roads)

11. As **Vicarage Lane** meets junction (green area in middle with wooden covered seat) go straight down towards octagonal structure (for toilets, turn *left* a few paces down street)

✓ *Don't miss seeing the attractive Sheepwash bridge and information board.*

12. Follow road round past **Holy Trinity Church** on left and later past **Bulls Head**

✓ *The church has an inlaid 'black marble' tabletop. Black marble is a highly polished type of limestone that Ashford was famous for in the 19th century.*

13. At junction by local shop and **Ashford Arms** turn *left* and after short distance turn *right* into **Hall End Lane**

14. At end of lane go through stile in wall to follow public footpath

15. Go through further stile, turn *left* and follow pavement (for approximately 3 minutes)

16. As road begins to curve left, cross over and enter footpath on right (entrance is easily missed, look out for 2 stone posts)

17. Go over stream, through gate and up woodland path

18. Go over stile, up field and over further stile

19. Head diagonally to top left hand corner of field, go over stile in wall by gateway and turn *left* (keep wall on left)

20. At hall, keep to path going diagonally across field towards gate and stile

21. Go over stile, turn *left* along lane and go through further gateway or stile. Turn *right* as lanes meet

22. On reaching main road, cross over and keep on towards **Great Longstone** (past gates)

23. Walk under bridge and a few paces beyond bridge turn *left* and cross stile

24. Shortly after, go through stile in wall on right and head along path (if you miss this stile you will end up on the **Monsal Trail**)

25. Continue along path (running parallel to road on right)

26. Go through stile in wall (**Great Longstone** now in view)

27. Go through further stile and across to gate. Through gate and follow path to road

28. Turn *right* down road (**Edge View Drive**)

29. At junction turn *right* and head down to main road. Turn *left* and follow main street past local shop and **White Lion** pub

30. Just before **The Crispin** pub turn *left* up **Station Road** (towards **Thornbridge Hall**)

31. After approx. 200m (**Orchard House** on left) turn *right* through stile in wall and follow path across field

32. Pass through 3 stiles with small gates to reach a wide track

33. Go straight across wide track, through stile in wall and continue across field to opposite right hand corner

34. Go over stile in corner and one more stile and continue down hill into **Little Longstone**

35. Go through gate or over stile, turn *left* and follow road past **Pack Horse Inn**, back to **Monsal Head Hotel** and car park

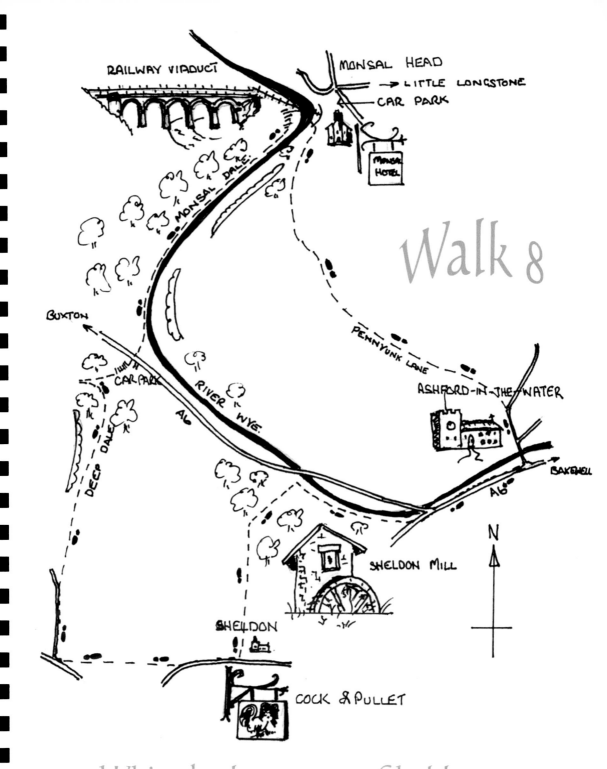

RAILWAY VIADUCT

MONSAL HEAD

→ LITTLE LONGSTONE

CAR PARK

MONSAL HOTEL

MONSAL DALE

Walk 8

BUXTON

PENNYUNK LANE

CAR PARK

ASHFORD-IN-THE-WATER

RIVER WYE

A6

DEEP DALE

BAKEWELL

A6

N

SHELDON MILL

SHELDON

COCK & PULLET

White Lodge car park - Sheldon

Ashford in the Water - Monsal Head

Walk 8

White Lodge car park - Sheldon - Ashford in the Water - Monsal Dale

About this walk

A slightly longer walk, but don't be discouraged by this as it is well worth the effort. You may consider taking a break for lunch at a village pub or eating a packed lunch at one of the many splendid viewpoints. This is a beautiful route encompassing a wide variety of landscapes, including river, woodland, dales, country villages and the spectacular Monsal Dale and viaduct.

Distance	14km.
Terrain	Shortly after starting the walk there is a short but fairly steep climb. Following this, the further rises are more gradual but the route includes a couple of steep descents, one of which is down a long set of steps leading to the river. The terrain is varied and includes tracks, pathways, steps, riverside and a short section along grass verges beside the road.
Map	OS Explorer OL24 The Peak District, White Peak area. 1:25 000 scale.
Starting Point	Car park situated approx. 3.5km West of Ashford in the Water, along the A6(T) towards Buxton (pay and display). Grid reference SK 171 705.
Refreshments	Sheldon village has an attractive pub (The Cock and Pullet) and Ashford in the Water offers pubs and teashop (limited opening). At Monsal Head there is an opportunity to admire the spectacular view, whilst taking advantage of refreshments offered by the café or hotel. In summer there is generally an ice cream van at this point.

1. Go through gateway above car park and 1 further gate, then follow path (ignore footpath to **Taddington** on your right at a very tiny bridge)

2. Continue along path over some rocks keeping to right of stream

3. Cross stream, go over stile and follow rocky path as it winds up the hill

4. When you come to a T-junction turn *right* towards **Deepdale** and **Monyash**

5. Carry on down to stream at bottom of path. Continue straight on (keep wall on right)

6. Eventually, when path reaches a wall in front, go through gate on right

7. Turn *left* and continue along path, keeping wall on your left (ignore stile about 80m further along on the left)

8. Go through gateway and continue straight on

9. When path meets a wall, go through small gate at side of a large one

10. Keep straight on along grassy lane, keeping same wall on your left (a bit further on ignore stiles opposite each other)

11. As lane meets road turn *left* and walk almost 100m to a stile and small gate on left

12. Pass through gate and bear about 45 degrees to right, towards stile in wall

13. Go through stile and across field towards a gateway in middle of opposite wall

14. Pass through gateway and cross field at slight angle to left, towards stile in wall ahead

15. Cross over stile and go across field (bearing slightly left)

✓ **The chimney and buildings of the disused Magpie lead mine can be seen silhouetted in the distance.**

16. Cross stile by gate next to fenced in dew pond (further left is a small farm building). At time of writing, stile due for construction by National Park, so if not there yet, use gate!

17. Walk straight across field towards a stile. Go over stile and walk diagonally to top left hand corner of field

18. Cross stile beside gateway and turn *left* along road towards **Sheldon**

19. Follow road as it curves right, past a farm and village hall

✓ **Just before the 'Cock and Pullet', notice the plaque on the wall giving information on SHELDON village.**

20. A short distance past pub take lane on your left (leading to church)

21. Carry on down lane past church (ignore right turn)

22. When you reach a gate and stile, turn *right* down narrow track (wall on both sides)

Magpie Mine

23. Go through very narrow stile and continue down path (with wall on your left)

24. Cross over wooden stile and continue down path

25. Cross over stile in wall and go straight up field (keeping wall on your right)

26. At end of field walk across to the large gate leading into a wood

27. Follow path straight down and keep following as it turns right down (rather a lot of!) steep steps

28. At bottom of steps turn *right* towards **Ashford** (you will see A6 road and some ponds on your left). Continue to follow path along river

29. Just after disused mill, ignore bridge, bear right and continue along river

30. Cross over stile by gateway and go straight on (keeping wall on your right)

31. Go over next stile or through gateway and continue along main track

32. Pass through small gate next to a large one and follow track to the road

33. On reaching road turn *left*, walk to T-junction with A6 and turn *right*

34. Keep to this side of road until you reach stone bridge opposite and then cross over bridge into **Ashford in the Water**

✓ **Note information board on wall at the village side of the bridge.**

35. Carry on to road, turn *left* and follow road up to junction (small green area in middle with covered wooden seat)

36. Continue straight up hill (**Vicarage Lane**)

37. Less than 100m on left hand side, go through some stone gate posts leading up a narrow path (this path will appear to turn you back)

38. Follow path as it turns you right, up some steps (keep houses on right)

39. Go through a narrow gap in wall and head straight on

40. Cross over stile and go straight across field, heading for stile in opposite wall

41. Go over this stile and turn *left* up lane (as you pass a cottage, ignore gate and footpath heading right). Continue along lane as it meanders for some distance

42. At end of track go through stone stile at side of gate, head straight up field (keeping wall on left)

43. At top of field go through little gate by a large one and turn *right*

44. Go on until you reach another small gate by a large one (with a dew pond on right)

45. Go through this small gate and continue along lane (with a wall on both sides)

46. Go through stile by large gate and walk on (with no wall on left hand side)

47. Go through next small gate at side of large one and continue along lane

48. The next small gate brings you to **Monsal Head**, with stunning views of the Dales

49. From this gate turn *right* and follow path down the hill, down steps and over next stile

50. Continue to steps, leading upwards to viewpoint (in front of hotel and café)

✓ **An excellent spot to take some refreshment while enjoying the views.**

51. From this point return through gap in wall, turn *right* and head down steps

52. At bottom of steps turn *left* and head downhill towards the viaduct

53. At bottom of pathway go through gate (there is a blocked entrance to a tunnel on your left) turn *right* and cross viaduct

54. On reaching far side of viaduct go through gate or stile on left and head down path towards river

55. Continue down path and turn *right* along riverside (away from viaduct)

56. Keep walking along riverside, past weir (stay on main track along river)

57. Ignore right turn to **Brushfield** near end of path. At end of path cross stile and small stream and head on up path

58. Go up steps and through gap in wall. Cross road to car park opposite

Ashford in the Water

Bakewell

Ashford in the Water

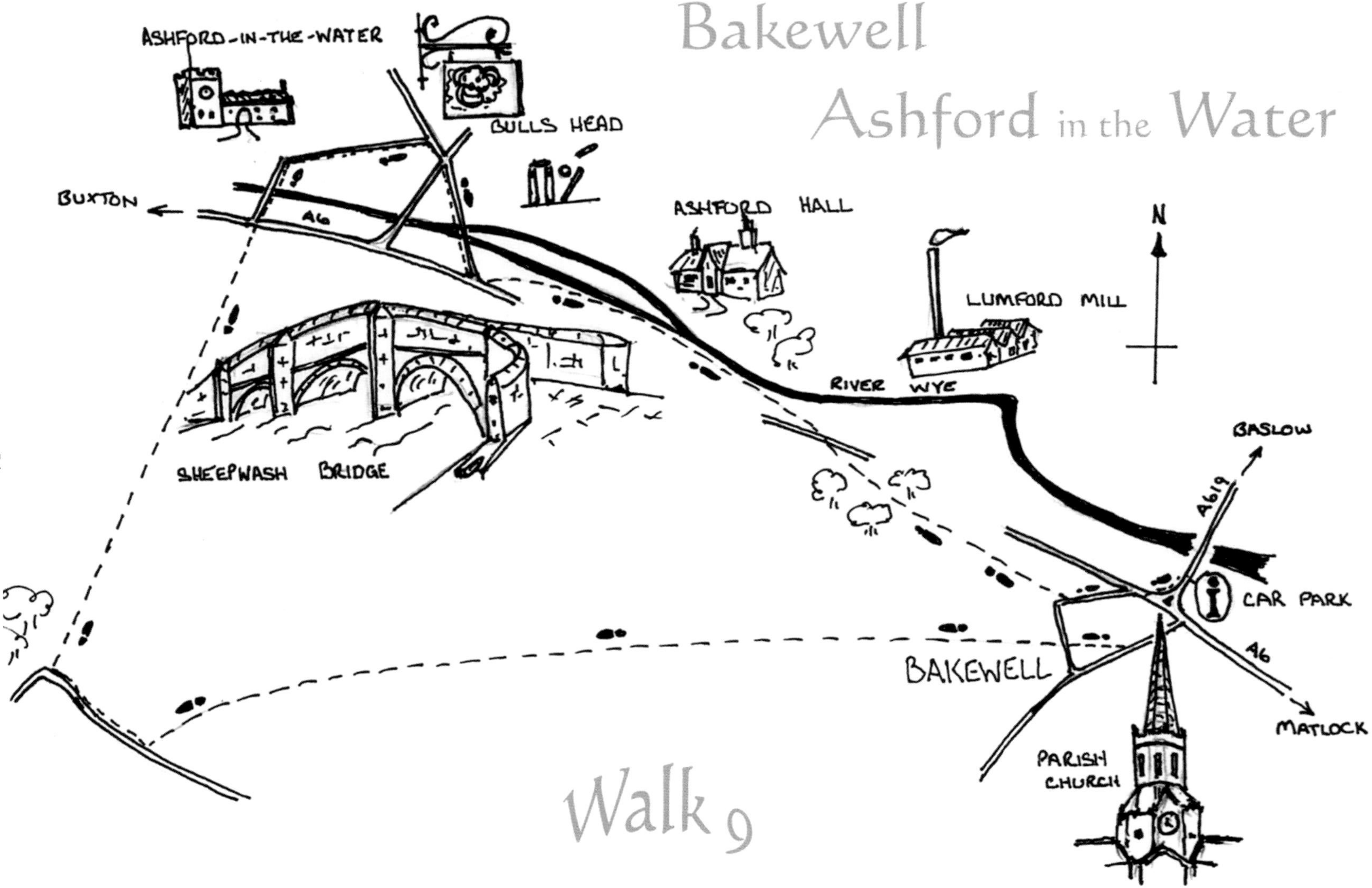

Walk 9

N

BASLOW

A619

CAR PARK

A6

MATLOCK

PARISH CHURCH

BAKEWELL

LUMFORD MILL

RIVER WYE

ASHFORD HALL

BULLS HEAD

ASHFORD-IN-THE-WATER

A6

BUXTON

SHEEPWASH BRIDGE

Walk 9

Bakewell - Ashford in the Water

About this walk

An interesting walk starting in a historic and thriving market town. This gives you the opportunity to explore the town as well as experiencing a very attractive country route to a picturesque village.

Distance	7.5km.
Terrain	Not too demanding, but a couple of climbs, including one towards the end of the walk, which is steepish but short. A good variety of terrain, including streets, fields, lanes, riverside, woodland and pathways.
Map	OS Explorer OL24 The Peak District, White Peak area. 1:25 000 scale.
Starting Point	Tourist Information Centre in Bridge Street, Bakewell. Grid reference SK 218 685. There are several car parks in and around the town.
Refreshments	Bakewell is a bustling market town, offering a good number of cafés, restaurants, pubs and fish and chip shops (look out for the original Bakewell Pudding shops). Ashford has several pubs and a café with limited opening hours.

1. From **Tourist Information Centre** walk along **Bridge Street** past the traffic lights towards **Rutland Arms Hotel**

2. Go up **King Street** (on left of hotel) and carry on up hill. Just past church, at first opening in wall, turn sharp *right* and then *left* up steps

3. At top of steps turn *right* and immediately *left* and follow lane up hill

4. As lane bears left, go straight on up narrow path, through small gate and continue up hill (wall on left)

5. Go through small gate and keep on as path bears left

6. Go through stile and small gate in corner of field, then take diagonal path towards far right hand of next field

7. Go through stile, continue along path as it bears slightly right to wall ahead

8. Go through gate and turn *left* onto lane. After a few paces, turn *right* over stile and follow path down (past stables)

9. Shortly, on reaching small copse on right, go over stile in wall on left and head down hill to stile in middle of bottom wall

10. Go down dip and up path to cross stile over to left

11. From stile go straight on (keeping wall on left)

12. Go over stile in corner of wall, cross lane and go over further stile opposite, leading through field (we were dwarfed by a tall maize crop here, but it was passable!)

13. Go across stile and straight on through line of trees, then over stile on wall to left

14. Continue through next line of trees and follow path uphill, heading for top right hand corner

15. Go up steps and across stile and turn *right* down lane. Follow this lane for about 1km (approximately 15 minutes)

16. As road bends left opposite mast on right, go through small gate on right and follow path down hill past mast (wall on right)

17. At corner of wall, carry on down hill towards **Ashford** (which can be seen in distance)

18. Next to cottage on right, path becomes lane. Follow this down through gate, across main road and over **Sheepwash Bridge** (for public toilets, go straight up **Fennel Street** and take first right)

✓ **At village side of bridge an information board can be seen.**

19. At bridge turn *right* and walk along **Church Street** past **Holy Trinity Church** on left

✓ **An example of an inlaid 'black marble' tabletop can be seen in church.**

20. Wind on through village.

21. Cross over to **Ashford Arms** side of road and continue round **Church Street** to main **A6020**

22. Cross main road and head down smaller road opposite (gate across and cricket ground to left)

23. Follow this road over bridge to main **A6 road**. Turn *left* along pavement

24. Very shortly (opposite houses) turn *left* through small gate and head *right* along river

25. Follow path along river, through 2 gates and 1 stile (path gradually moves away from river)

26. Go over further stile and along path between houses

27. On reaching road, go straight across and along another narrow path between houses

28. Go over stile and follow path ahead

29. Go through stile by gate and turn *left* along pavement

❖ **If you wish to cut short your walk, continue down main road into Bakewell (approximately 1km).**

30. Just past (Deepdale) **Business Park** on right, cross road and enter **Endcliff Wood**

31. Go up path to top of hill in wood and carry straight on (ignore path to right)

32. As path opens onto school playing fields, turn *right* and head down right side of building

33. At end of this building turn *right*, go through school exit and *left* down **Stanedge Road**

34. Follow road as it curves left and at next junction turn *right* (ignore **Fly Hill**)

35. Follow road down past church and into town centre. At roundabout carry straight on for **Tourist Information Centre**

The Hathersage Walks

North Lees Hall

Hathersage Church Lych-gate

Ruin of Catholic Chapel

Little John's Grave

HERE LIES BURIED
LITTLE JOHN
THE FRIEND & LIEUTENANT OF
ROBIN HOOD
HE DIED IN A COTTAGE (NOW DESTROYED)
TO THE EAST OF THE CHURCHYARD
THE GRAVE IS MARKED BY
THIS OLD HEADSTONE & FOOTSTONE
AND IS UNDERNEATH THIS OLD YEW TREE

The Needle Girl's Tale

If I'm going to end up like my mother (and I probably am, why fool myself?) then I'm going to make sure I enjoy a bit of my life first.

Let me tell you about my mother. She must be thirty-six, which is old enough, but she looks a deal older. She's got six children still living and a face that no man's going to take a second glance at. Hard to imagine anyone ever did, but she tells me she had the pick of Hathersage at eighteen, not that it probably amounted to much, not if it's anything like now. She picked my Pa, and it turned out to be a very bad choice because he was drunk for much of the time and shouting at us the rest. That's how I remember it, anyway. He died two years ago - grinders disease, people said. I doubt you've ever heard of such a thing, so I'll tell you more of it in a moment.

I never mourned him and I'm sure she didn't either, even though we needed some help from that Poor Law Relief to get by. She did a bit of needle packing at home, but that didn't bring much in. Work done at home is even worse paid than here, and in any case she couldn't do a great deal with children around and a lot of other work to do. I was the oldest and I'd already been at work here a while. I was more than glad to be out of that schoolroom up the street. I'd had enough of reading, writing and adding up and the schoolmistress had probably had enough of me. I wasn't her favourite pupil. Now most of what I earn goes to help feed the family. They need every penny I make, but they don't get it. I make sure I put a few coins each week into a box, and I keep that box well hidden. You've got to look after yourself.

Started here just before my thirteenth birthday - summer of 1842 - and since then I've been packing things - needles, hackle pins, gill pins - whatever it is that's sent into this back room from the factory through there. You wouldn't believe how many needles people must buy. Some are even sent to foreign places, like France. Me and Doris have to put them all into little packets and then we wrap the best ones in fancy paper. Of course hackles and gill pins are used in the making of wool, and that's a very big industry nowadays.

There's hardly any women working in this place, and I'm the only girl here. It's nearly all boys and men - and no worse for that! Nice to get the eye when you walk through the workshops, and there's a good few of them that find some reason to come in here. They'll bring a box of pins, or something that got left behind, so they tell me. I know it's nonsense. One or two older men aren't above that sort of thing either. I don't bother to smile or say thank you unless it's someone I have a fancy for, and there's not so many of those. But I know it's me they want to see. Doris is well past being looked at - she's nearly thirty - and other than us there's only daft Joseph around the back here. He's not up to doing a proper man's job, like wire pulling or needle grinding. Course he's not paid much for just stacking boxes or loading them up onto carts out in the yard - mostly boxes filled with the little packets of needles that me and Doris have made up and then wrapped. We can do it almost without looking, and very fast too, if there's any one around that matters. Mr Cook is might marry in a year or two, if nothing better comes my way. He's a grinder, like Pa was - there's a fair number of grinders in this place as well, but it's better that he's not been taken on here, right under my feet. Gives me a chance to keep my eyes open, and is there any reason why I shouldn't? After all, we're not married yet and life probably won't be much fun when we are. Once babies start to come, it's nothing but work and worries, isn't it? But I don't want to end up an old maid either, like Doris, that's much worse.

To be honest, John's not badly paid for the job he does, he's as well paid as anyone's going to be in this sort of place. The grinders would be a great deal better off if they didn't drink most of their wages! Course it's a very skilled job, grinding, not many can master it. A lot of boys try to learn when they reach fifteen or sixteen, but most of them never do it well enough. You've to hold fifty or more needle wires between your two hands, all placed out flat and straight. Then you need to roll them, not letting any drop, and at the same time push all the ends against the grindstone, which is what gets them sharp. If your fingers catch the stone it can rip the skin of them. Of course the grindstone's turning very very fast, so dust and grit and tiny bits of steel are all flying off right up into your face. All that stuff gets in your mouth and down your throat, but the windows are kept tight shut and they're covered with sticky dust, so it's quite dark in there as well. That's why my Pa used to drink so much. He said he had to, or else his throat was dry and sore all the time and he could neither eat nor sleep. As I said, they all drink a lot, the grinders - when they're not working they're in The George or some other alehouse. John takes less than most of them, but then he's still trying to make sure of me. When he has, I don't doubt he'll be just like the rest.

Not long back they gave John some sort of mouth cover with a face screen fixed on it, but he doesn't use it - hardly any of them do. He says he'd rather tie a handkerchief round, and in any case the grinders all say they get paid well on account of it being such a bad job to do. If it wasn't so bad, there wouldn't be the same money in it.

Mind you, we all have to breathe in a lot of that dust and grit. The whole village is covered in the damn stuff and you can smell the black smoke coming out of this place from a good distance off. But the grinding room's the worst of all. I've only been in a couple of times but I could scarcely breathe.

John's a good grinder. He can sharpen up thousands of needle wires in an hour. He's even hoping to get Mr Cocker - that's the owner of Atlas Works - to pay him a shilling a week more. That would give us a decent wage to live on, even with children. What worries me, though, is that John's always coughing up and he's sick more often than most. It's a nasty colour, the phlegm he coughs up, dark brown and thick looking. He says it's nothing that a drink and a bit of fresh air won't cure, but sometimes of a summer evening when we get out for a walk on the hills, he tires quite soon. Well I know that's often an excuse to make sure the two of us get lying down in some quiet spot together - he's not so ill that he doesn't want to do things like that. If it was down to him, there'd no doubt be one on its way already, and then we'd have to be married quicker than I'd choose. But it seems to me he doesn't have a strong look about him, not like some of the other ones I take notice of. And there's no grinder I know of that's more than forty and very few as old as that. Still, I suppose forty's not so young. It's a very long way off - John's barely twenty.

Must get on now. Work's been slow coming in today, but there's another lot of pins just arrived and I'm told they're to be ready and packed up by tonight, so they can be sent across by horse and cart to Bradford tomorrow. Must be going to some woollen mill.

Take a look around Hathersage while you're here. It's fairly clean now and I don't doubt it smells sweeter. Any dirt in the air these days is from cars, not from the making of goods. I doubt if anyone makes anything here any more. You could walk as far as North Lees Hall - of course the Eyres have all gone now and so have the servants. I'm told rich people stay there for holidays, so in some ways things haven't changed so much. That Brontë woman wrote a book and put North Lees Hall in it - Thornfield Hall, she called it. She used the name Eyre in the book as well.

Whatever it is you're doing around these parts, make sure you enjoy yourself. Life's short, and in my experience most of it's very hard.

Photograph - by kind permission of Matlock local studies library

Walk 10

GREEN'S HOUSE

CAR PARK

WC

NORTH LEES

BRONTE COTTAGE

BROOKFIELD MANOR

HOOD BROOK

N

HATHERSAGE

North Lees Hall - Hathersage

Green's House

Walk 10

North Lees Hall - Hathersage - Green's House

About this walk

A real must this one! Definitely one of our favourite walks. North Lees Hall, once visited by Charlotte Brontë and reputed to be the inspiration for 'Thornfield Hall' in 'Jane Eyre', is a charming building in a beautiful setting. You will enjoy stunning views of the Edges, whilst walking through a great variety of beautiful countryside, including meadows, woodlands, hillside and valley. There is an opportunity to visit Hathersage if you wish (about half way along the route).

Distance	6km.
Terrain	Not a demanding walk. The only significant ascent comes towards the end of the walk, but it is only a gradual pull. Paths are generally well defined and reasonably easy underfoot.
Map	OS Explorer OL1 The Peak District, Dark Peak area. 1:25 000 scale.
Starting Point	Approaching Hathersage from the East on A6187. As you enter Hathersage turn right into School Lane (past Scotsmans Pack Inn). After about 1.5 miles, as road bears sharp right, turn left and continue along until road splits. Then bear right. Parking is on right just past toilets on left. Grid reference SK 237 838.
Refreshments	Hathersage has a good number of cafés, pubs and shops.

1. Turn *left* from car park and walk as far as building on right of road (Peak National Park Ranger Briefing Centre and public toilets). Cross over the road

2. Take footpath at far side of this building and follow it down towards stream

3. When path meets a lane, turn *right* and continue down lane

4. Go over a stile at a gate and carry on down hill

5. Go through a gate, walk a few paces, turn *left*

✓ **Note the information plaques, one set in a stone at the side of North Lees Hall, the other set in a wall at the front of the Hall.**

6. Follow lane past front of Hall, go through a gate and continue down drive

7. Go through a gate at bottom of drive, turn *left* and walk along road

8. Just past **North Lees Campsite** (on left) turn *right* up bank at side of road. Cross stile and head along track

9. Go through small gate to left of farm buildings and follow track round buildings

10. Continue up track, going through 2 gates (further on, ignore gateway on right)

11. Go over stile in corner of field and head down, passing through some wooden posts

12. Continue to follow path down as it bears left and joins another path

13. Just before next corner, ignore path to right, cross stream and go up earthen steps

14. At top of steps turn *right*, go across stile and straight up (keeping graveyard on right)

15. Go through lych-gate on right to arrive at front of Parish Church of **St. Michael and All Angels**

✓ A Lych-gate is a roofed gateway of a churchyard where traditionally a coffin awaited the clergyman's arrival.

✓ Opposite main door of church, a sign points to the grave of 'Little John', friend and lieutenant of Robin Hood.

16. Go past church entrance and continue down churchyard

✓ Note the view of Hathersage in its lovely setting.

17. At end of churchyard, go through gate, turn *left* and immediately *right* through another gate

18. Follow path down (a high wall on left) and go through 2 more gates

19. At bottom of path go through a gate and turn *right*

❖ If you would like to walk into Hathersage, turn left at this gate and follow the lane for a few minutes to reach the town. Then return and continue from this point.

North Lees Hall

64

20. Go through gate by cattle grid and continue along lane through a meadow (passing 3 more gates)

21. Shortly before a farm, bear left towards **Brookfield Manor**

✓ *The manor was built in the 17th century on the site of an old Catholic seminary, where priests stayed on their way to and from the continent.*

22. Go through gate and along narrow path (with a hedge on left)

23. Walk past **Brookfield Manor** buildings and on reaching the road, go straight across and over a stile

24. Follow winding path across a meadow to wall opposite

25. Go through small gate into '**The Warren**' and continue along path

✓ *This is a woodland regeneration area.*

26. Cross bridge on left and follow path up the hill

27. Go over stile and across field to reach gate in wall

28. Carry on up to stile at top of field

✓ *Look back for a wonderful view across the valley.*

29. Walk along path, through hole in wall, and turn *right* into grassy lane

✓ *The view ahead is Stanage Edge and on many fine days climbers and hang gliders can be seen here.*

30. At gateway at end of lane, bear diagonally right to go down to stile by another gateway (farm building is in distance ahead)

31. Go over stile and continue down to further stile by gate

✓ *The ruins of Green's House Mill, dam and mill pond are beside Hood Brook. There was a lead smelting mill here in the early 18th century which was converted to a paper mill in about 1760.*

32. Follow track as it winds down to stream, cross over stream and stile and continue uphill

✓ *Note the ruined archway of a former Catholic chapel, on the right.*

33. Keep to path (ignore gate on right). As path joins grassy track, continue going up (keeping farm buildings on right)

34. At the top of track, just past gate, go over stile

35. Follow path straight down the hill (do not turn right towards Hall). Path eventually curves round to left to meet gate and stile leading into wood

36. Go over stile and walk up lane. Near the top of lane, take flight of stone steps on left, to reach toilets and Ranger Briefing Centre

37. Turn *left* and walk along road, to return to car park on right

about at times - he's the owner of this manufactory - and then you wouldn't believe how fast our fingers move. Other times we slow down a bit and have a gossip, but we're never too slow because they count the boxes going out of here at the end of each day. Mr Cook wouldn't be able to have his big house and his servants if he stood for any idleness, now would he? Barnfield House, it's called. We walked past it once, me and John, and I thought - no wonder we all have to work so hard. Six o'clock till six o'clock I'm in this room, and later if there's anything to be got out quickly. My fingers ache all night, once I stop. And they're covered in little cuts and scabs. We get a bit of a rest in the middle of the day, and I go out to the yard with my hunk of bread and bit of ham or bacon, and see if there's any one there worth chatting to.

No, I wouldn't say I enjoy it here, it's too hard and the day's too long, but at least I'm no one's servant and there's little work around for girls other than that. My friend Lizzie works as a maid over at North Lees Hall - that's another rich house not far from here. Lizzie's 16, like me, and she lives in. She has to make an even earlier start to the day than I do. A family called Eyre lives in that place, been there for a very long time, and at the moment there's a Mrs Eyre, with four of her children. None of them married and three of them over forty - can you imagine? Even the youngest is thirty-nine! Lizzie says Mrs Eyre is nice enough, but of course she doesn't see much of her, it's some miserable housekeeper that has her eye on Lizzie all day long and never stops finding fault. She has to be polite all the time, and do everything just so. I wouldn't be able to abide that. I like to speak my mind plainly, and you can say just what you think to people in this place. It wouldn't suit any one too fussy because you hear foul language often enough - though not when Mr Cook's around, he doesn't stand for it.

Of course Lizzie sometimes sees the sort of people I never come across. A woman was there a few weeks back, quite a well known person, Lizzie said, a writer - not that I'd ever heard of her. Brontë, she was called - odd name, that's why it's stuck in my mind. Arrived there with her friend from the vicarage - Ellen Nussey - and they were borrowing a horse from Mrs Eyre. Lizzie was out in the yard emptying something when they were getting it saddled up. "Do take your time, Charlotte," pipes Mrs Eyre, "and have a lovely day, my dear." Must be very nice to have the time to take! Those sort of people don't know what it's like in places like this. It's not their world, is it? Lizzie says that Ellen has often been to the Hall, and not long ago she overheard her chatting to Mrs Eyre while she was laying out some tea for them. Ellen's brother is the vicar in Hathersage, and Ellen was saying he'd once proposed to this Charlotte Brontë! She turned him down, and now he's gone off and married someone else - someone quite rich. Anyway, Lizzie didn't think Charlotte looked the marrying sort, any more than this Ellen does. Very prim and proper, both of them, and none too young either.

There's plenty of men here in this factory of Mr Cook's. Some of them came in from other places with their families and the village has grown a bit since my mother was young. This isn't the only manufactory here - there's four others in the village, all making much the same sort of thing as we do - wires, pins, needles, even umbrella frames. At one time, a long way back, this village was famous for making brass buttons - that was in Dale Mill. But nobody seems to want brass buttons now, so Dale Mill makes needles and pins, like the rest of us. The Atlas Works is just down the road and that's where John is, the one I

Walk II

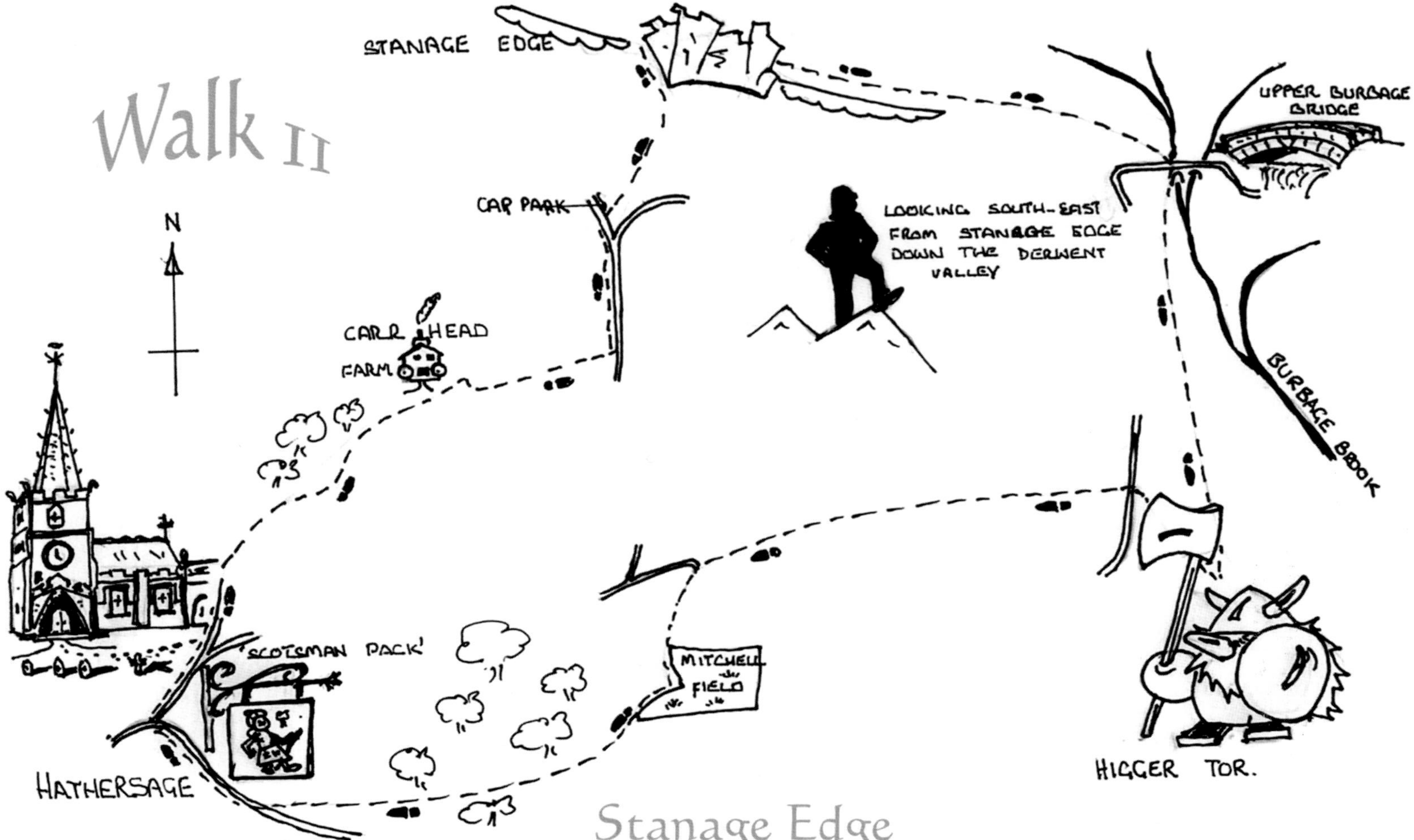

STANAGE EDGE
CAR PARK
N
CARR HEAD
FARM
LOOKING SOUTH-EAST
FROM STANAGE EDGE
DOWN THE DERWENT
VALLEY
UPPER BURBAGE
BRIDGE
BURBAGE BROOK
SCOTSMAN PACK'
MITCHELL
FIELD
HATHERSAGE
HIGGER TOR.

Stanage Edge

Higger Tor

Hathersage

Walk 11

Stanage Edge - Higger Tor - Hathersage

About this walk

The views from this walk are quite spectacular. Your route takes you along the dramatic Stanage Edge and the high point of Higger Tor. You will also have the opportunity to visit Hathersage, if you wish (about two-thirds the way along the route).

Distance	9km.
Terrain	A slightly more demanding walk, well rewarded by its views and scenery. A short but fairly steep ascent onto the Edge from the parking area at the start. From Hathersage a gradual uphill walk with one steepish pull towards the end. A mixture of paths, tracks, lanes and pavements. A lot of rocky paths and can be muddy.
Map	OS Explorer OL1 The Peak District, Dark Peak area. 1:25 000 scale.
Starting Point	Approaching Hathersage from East on A6187. As you enter Hathersage turn right into School Lane (go past Scotsmans Pack Inn). After about 1.5 miles, just before road bears right, go over cattle grid, turn left and parking is immediately on right. Grid reference SK 244 829.
Refreshments	Hathersage has a good number of cafés, pubs and shops.

1. From top end of parking area (to right of rock face ahead) go through gap in wall

2. Follow path up the hill, as it leads up to right hand side of rock face

3. When path forks, bear to right (left fork leads to rock face)

4. At top, turn *right* and follow rocky, well defined path along **Stanage Edge**

5. Eventually, go up to triangulation pillar (small concrete pillar with metal strips in top). A few paces past pillar, turn *left* and follow a well defined stone slab path down

6. As path drops steeply down, head towards clearly visible path below, which leads across moorland (**Burbage Edge** is ahead and to right)

7. Walk along path until you reach road, cross road, turn *left* and head towards bridge

8. Just before bridge, enter car park at main entrance and cross stile on left

9. Turn *right* and take upper of two paths heading across the hill (keep **Burbage Edge**, which is across the valley, on left)

10. Keep heading up rocky path, which will eventually go quite steeply downhill

11. Continue along a well defined path leading across to **Higger Tor**, which lies ahead (a wood lies down in valley on left)

✓ Higger Tor (large rocky hill) is thought to be a Viking burial ground. The name is probably a corruption of the name of a Viking god.

12. As path reaches top of **Higger Tor**, it will join another path coming up from road

❖ **If you wish to explore Higger Tor and its stunning views, carry straight on and then return here to continue from point 13.**

13. Turn *right* and head downwards to road

14. Go over stile, cross road, turn *right* and walk a few paces to stile on left

15. Cross stile, walk straight ahead for about 45 steps to point where paths cross

16. Turn *left* and follow path going down the hill (farm buildings will soon come into view in valley)

17. Where path meets track, cross stile, turn *right* and head down track

18. Go through a gateway (ruined building is on right) and continue to head down

19. As track reaches bottom of hill turn *left* just before small bridge, to **Mitchell Field Farm**

20. Ignore footpath on right (before farm) and follow track around left side of buildings

21. At end of buildings, ignore footpath on left and continue on, as track bears left away from buildings

22. After just a few paces, turn *right* across grass to join very narrow path leading down a dip and up through trees to a wall

23. Go over stile in wall, take diagonal route to right across field, to next stile in wall

Brontë Cottage (Walk 10)

68

24. Cross this stile and head up the hill, keeping wall on left but walking slightly to the right, through middle of this large field

25. Path soon leads over the hill to boundary wall of an impressive stone house

26. On reaching wall, turn *left* and follow path around front of house

27. By house gate, join drive leading away from house

28. As drive curves to left, carry straight on along grassy path (keeping wall on right)

29. Go over stile and continue down towards wood

30. After a few paces turn *left* (ignore gateway ahead) and drop down dip to cross stile on right

31. Walk along a narrow path in wood (there is a wall on left)

32. Eventually main path turns left, keep to this main path and carry on down (do not continue straight on towards a gate that leads out of wood)

33. Go through rickety gate (if it's still there!) and head down path (as path becomes a lane, it passes a number of houses on left)

34. At end of lane, cross main road, turn *right* and walk down hill towards **Hathersage**

35. As road rounds bend into town, cross road, turn *right* and walk along **School Lane**

❖ **If you wish to visit Hathersage Town, do not turn right into School Lane, but carry straight on. To rejoin walk, return to School Lane.**

36. Just opposite '**Scotsmans Pack**' go *left* up steep road (**Church Bank**) towards Church

✓ **The church is worth a visit, and in the graveyard is Little John's (alleged) grave.**

37. At fork in road, bear right up a private road (if you reach church you've missed it!) Follow this road up as it turns sharp left and continue up (ignore gate on left further on)

38. Keep to main lane. Later ignore narrow path on right and go over cattle grid, past gate post and head up towards farm

39. Go through gate and walk past **Carr Head Farm**

40. Just before next gateway and cattle grid (leading to **Moorseats Hall**) turn *right* up the hill to wall opposite (ignore stile a few paces up on left)

41. Go through gate at top left, turn *right* and head straight up field (farm at your back)

42. Carry on up steep field for about three quarters of the way, then turn *right* (through remains of stone wall) and walk diagonally towards large gate in wall

43. Go through gate and head straight up. After short distance, bear left through stone gateposts, then immediately *right* along surfaced lane

44. When lane meets road, turn *left* and walk up road

45. Just past cattle grid, turn *left* and walk down to car parking area

Walk 12

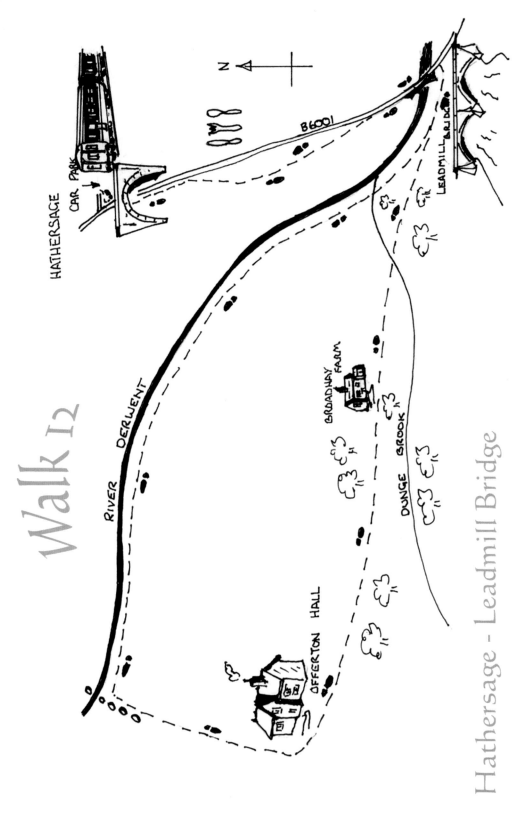

HATHERSAGE

CAR PARK

B6001

N

LEADMILL BRIDGE

RIVER DERWENT

BROADHAY FARM

DUNGE BROOK

OFFERTON HALL

Hathersage - Leadmill Bridge

Riverside (Derwent) - Offerton

Walk 12

Hathersage - Leadmill Bridge - Riverside (Derwent) - Offerton

About this walk

A fairly leisurely but very attractive walk from Hathersage, partly along the riverside. Lovely views on the way, and stunning at times. A mix of riverside, woodlands, fields and the attractive Offerton Hall (private residence).

Distance	6.5km.
Terrain	One slightly demanding hill leading up to Offerton Hall, but well worth taking a breather to look at the 'breathtaking' views behind. A variety of terrains, with narrow paths at times, but fairly even underfoot.
Map	OS Explorer OL1 The Peak District, Dark Peak area. 1:25 000 scale.
Starting Point	Car parking by Hathersage Station (up Station Approach) off B6001. Grid reference SK 232 810.
Refreshments	Hathersage has a good number of cafés, pubs and shops.

1. From car park exit go straight back along road **(Station Approach)**

2. When this meets main road, cross over and turn *left*

3. Pass under bridge and continue along pavement

✓ **You will shortly see 'The Round Building' on left which is a David Mellor cutlery and country shop.**

4. Opposite The Round Building go through stile on right and then straight across to opposite side of field. Turn *left* as you join well defined path

5. Continue on path until it meets main road, then through small gate and gap in wall

6. Turn *right* and follow pavement over **Leadmill Bridge**.

7. At far side of bridge turn *right* through stile in wall and small gate

8. Follow path along river (there may be stiles at certain points if repairs are done)

9. Eventually go through small gate into **Goose Nest Wood** and continue along path

10. Cross small bridge to the right and continue along riverside

11. Pass another bridge and a number of wooden gates (at time of writing - 9!)

12. When you see stepping stones crossing river, turn *left* and follow path up the hill towards **Offerton** (within a few metres **Offerton Hall** comes into view)

13. Half way up hill, go through gate (or over stile) and continue up

14. Go through next gate (or over stile) near Hall and continue

15. Go through gate alongside Hall and turn *left* up lane (**Offerton Hall** on left and **Offerton House** on right)

Stepping Stones, River Derwent

16. Follow lane as it winds up hill (ignore 2 footpaths on right)

17. About a further 300m along, just past a gateway on left, cross stile on left and turn *right* following path along hillside (gradually descending)

18. Cross small stream and stile and continue past houses on left

19. At end of path turn *left*, go down through gate by **Callow House Farm**

20. Head down through gap in wall and steps, bearing slightly right across field and through gate in wall (leading into wood)

21. Follow path down through wood and finally leave wood through gate

22. Follow track down to further gate in hedge and turn *right* up lane

23. As lane meets surfaced road (2 driveways on right) go through small gate on left

24. Turn *right* and follow path down hill to wall at corner of wood and continue on (with wood on left)

25. Go through gate (or over stile) and continue as path leads down

26. As wall starts on left, go over stile (you can now see river on left)

27. Follow path going down to right and at bottom of slope go straight on to river

28. At river bear right and head back to road, then go through gate and stile in wall and turn *left* over bridge

29. Follow pavement, passing under railway bridge, and turn *right* into **Station Approach** to reach car park